ABOUT

THOSE

SPECIAL

DAYS

By W. Hamp Watson, Jr.

CWP

Cambridge Way Publishing

Macon, Georgia

PLACING AN ORDER

Order from W. Hamp Watson, Jr. 149 Cambridge Way, Macon, Ga. 31220.

THE SALES PRICE: $10.00

Proceeds from all sales will benefit Mulberry United Methodist's Macon Outreach, a five day a week feeding Ministry with the poor and homeless of Macon, Georgia. If purchased at a United Methodist Church of the South Georgia Conference or an institution of the Conference, there will be no additional charge. Add $3.00 for a total of $13.00 including shipping and handling if ordered from W. Hamp Watson, Jr. Please make out the check to Macon Outreach.

Cover design by Lillian Davis

Scripture references are footnoted, but reference no particular version. Most often the public domain King James Version is used.

ABOUT THOSE SPECIAL DAYS

 For information, address Cambridge Way Publishing, 149 Cambridge Way, Macon, Ga. 31220-8736

ISBN 978-0-9746976-8-0

Also by W. Hamp Watson, Jr.

Frederick Wilson Still Speaks – Big Words for our Time, benefiting the SGC Methodist Homes for Children and Youth.

More Big Words for our Time, benefiting Wesley Glen, SGC Homes for Adults with Disabilities.

Little Stories/Big Ideas, benefiting The League of the Good Samaritan at Magnolia Manor, SGC homes for the aged.

A Christmas Cornucopia, benefiting "Miss Ella's Camp for Special People" at Epworth By the Sea.

Saying Yes and Amen to Life, benefiting The Vashti Center at Thomasville, Georgia, for disturbed children and young adults.

A Light Unto My Path, benefiting Open Door Community House in Columbus, Georgia.

Experiencing Ineffable Mystery, benefiting Wesley Community Centers in Savannah, Georgia.

All but one of the books above may be ordered by sending a check for $13.00 (covers postage also) for each book to:

W. Hamp Watson, Jr.
149 Cambridge Way
Macon, Georgia 31220-8736
478-475-1763
whwatson2@cox.net

The exception to this is $17 for *Little Stories/Big Ideas*.

$10 will be forwarded to the respective institution listed above for each book sold.

FOREWORD

When the title for this little volume says, "About Those Special Days," it is speaking of most of the Special Sundays or other "Special" days that are celebrated in most of the churches of South Georgia. It is not limited to the Official Lectionary Church Year, but also includes those Sundays and other special days that are celebrated. For instance, the preachers and pastors that would neglect such days as Valentine's Day or Church School Promotion Sunday or Independence Day/July the 4th or Mother's Day would soon find themselves in trouble. About half of the messages in this volume pertain to these days that are not listed in any Church Lectionary.

I have included one Jewish Special Day, the Feast of Booths or the Feast of Tabernacles as it is sometimes called. It focuses on the remembrance with gratitude of the Booths or tents or Tabernacles that the Jews used as dwelling places on their journey to escape the Egyptian bondage. This day is celebrated near the end of September or the beginning of October. It is fitting that it be included in a Christian book, for it speaks of our common heritage since the Old Testament is Christian History. We often celebrate this tie that binds as Rabbis come to our family nights to explain the meaning of Passover, Hanukah, Yom Kippur and other high holy days. Christian pastors visit Temples and Synagogues in return.

I offer these messages, portions of which might be used by pastors as they prepare for their own celebration of these days. I am also hopeful that you readers will find an idea here and there that illuminates these days and makes them more special for you.

W. Hamp Watson, Jr.

ACKNOWLEDGEMENTS

*The Reverend Tommy Martin, Senior Pastor of Mulberry United Methodist Church in Macon, Georgia, and now The Rev. Tommy Mason who has cooperated in many ways for the publication of this book to Benefit Macon Outreach, a five day per week feeding ministry for the poor in downtown Macon.

*The generous donors who are raising the $5,000+ amount required for printing and publicity so that Macon Outreach could benefit 100% from all sales of the book.

*All those volunteer laypersons in local churches who will take on the task of selling a consignment of books to their friends and fellow church members.

*The Rev. C. G. Haugabook and Allene Haugabook for proofreading and making other needed suggestions for improvement of the final version.

*Mrs. Sharon Pirkle (David) who placed Chapter Headers at the top of each page.

*Lillian Davis, Director of Publications for the Georgia Farm Bureau Mutual Insurance Company, for designing the front and back covers.

*Whitehall Printing Company of Naples, Florida, for a reasonable production cost.

*The faithful staffs of Macon Outreach and all volunteers in local churches in Macon and beyond that gather food supplies so that this vital ministry can continue.

W. Hamp Watson, Jr.

TABLE OF CONTENTS

REMEMBRANCE, RECKONING AND RESOLUTIONS
I Corinthians 11:23-26 Holy Communion

The burden of this brief message is how the New Year and the Lord's Supper are alike. But, more than that, I want to say that the Lord's Supper adds a deeper dimension of meaning at every point where they are alike.

For instance, they are both a time of remembrance. The New Year is a reminder of our limited years, or our limited life span—a time when we remember the things that we meant to do, but haven't done. Another year and the light in the bathroom isn't fixed. Time has passed and more of our dreams are not realized. In the old movie, A Song of the South, Uncle Remus sadly leaves the plantation after he was run off for telling wild stories to the children. He looked around the old, broken-down cabin in which he had lived and said to the little boy at his side, "I was going to get around to whitewashing these walls one o' these days."

A New Year can be a time of regret. An elderly man came to Dante Gabriel Rosetti with some sketches on which he wanted a judgment. He said, "Monsieur Rosetti, are these valuable? Is there any hope that I might succeed as an artist?"

Rosetti was tenderhearted and it hurt him to have to say it, but he said to the old man, "I am so sorry, but I'm afraid that they are worthless on any market. I would not encourage you to continue. You can only be disappointed, unless, of course, you only want to amuse yourself."

Then the old man laid before him some sketches that he said were done by a student. When he saw them, Rosetti said, "Oh, these are magnificent. Where is this young man? He should be encouraged in every way!"

The old man's face fell as he said, "Oh, Monsieur Rosetti, I was that student."

Of all sad words of tongue or pen,
The saddest are these, "It might have been."

The New Year is a time of remembrance, and often, regret.

But while the Lord's Supper is also a time of remembrance in which Christ reminds us, "Do this in remembrance of me," this is a time of remembrance that leads beyond regret to repentance. Knowing that our sin helped to put Christ on the cross ratchets regret up to a new level. The great Quaker mystic, Rufus Jones, had a younger brother who accidentally caught his hand in the blade of a mowing machine. Two fingers were cut off. The night after the accident, the boy kept the whole family awake by crying out again and again, "Oh, I wish I hadn't done it; I wish I hadn't done it!"

True repentance is the act in which you look at your true nature and see everything you've done to separate yourself from God and then cry out, "Oh, I wish I hadn't done it; I wish I hadn't done it!" It's more than just being sorry for your sins. It's the desire to cease being sorry as a person. And truly remembering Christ puts you on this path.

Henry Crane said, "People become like the thoughts they harbor, like the memories they cherish." The proverb said, "As you think in your heart, so are you." To remember Him, to cherish the thought of him, is to harbor heaven in your heart. When Jesus wanted to bless the world, he told us to think of, to remember Him, for it's what we remember that really blesses. Just like it's what we save and not what we earn that truly enriches. If you want the mind to be in you that was in Christ Jesus, you have to remember him. Then you find yourself purifying yourself, as he was pure. Through remembrance—repentance and change become possible. The New Year and the Lord's Supper are alike in that they're both a time of remembrance. One might bring regret, but the other can bring repentance and the chance for a new life.

And, the New Year and the Lord's Supper are both a time of reckoning. The New Year is a time of reckoning to our government of how we sold the goods that we had in our stores; we all take inventory. It's a time of reckoning as to how we earned and spent money. We make out our income tax returns. We take stock of ourselves in relation to our government and the tax that we owe to the government.

The Lord's Supper goes a step further. It's a time of reckoning too, but we reckon not just to the government but also to God. We give account of how we are spending our lives. What do we have in stock in the store of life? We confess our sin saying, "We have not loved you with our whole heart. We have failed to be an obedient church. We have not done your will, we have broken your law, we have rebelled against your love, we have not loved our neighbors, and we have not heard the cry of the needy." But in the Lord's Supper, we have to go beyond the general reckoning of our sins to personal and individual accounting in which we ask, "Is it I, Lord?" We let God have a clear look at our lives, completely honest in the accounting.

Some people are awfully afraid of the government—afraid that they might make a mistake and get caught for dishonesty in their reporting on their income tax return. But they are very little concerned to find a time when they are completely honest with God. We might as well, though. Jesus said, "Nothing is covered up that will not be uncovered, and nothing secret that will not become known." If we confess our sins, if we are completely honest in our time of reckoning, we need have no fear. "If we confess our sins, he who is faithful and just will forgive us our sins and cleanse us from all unrighteousness." The New Year and the Lord's Supper are alike in that they are both a time of reckoning.

They are also alike in that they are both a time for resolutions. I guess the most striking thing about New Year's resolutions is that they are most often made against the background of failure. Like the guy said,
"I can't see why I bother to make them,
As sure as I am that I'm going to break them."
Woman had a lawyer draw up her will. She bequeathed large amounts to a long list of churches and charities.

Amazed lawyer said, "Where do you have all this money?"

She said, "I don't really have it. I'm just doing this to show my good intentions."
Maybe this is just an honest analysis of the power of resolutions made only in our own strength. The Christian message is not an exhortation, "Try harder to be good." That's good advice, but there's no saving gospel in that.

The Lord's Supper furnishes the opportunity to make resolutions, too. Remember the invitation to come, "If you intend to lead a new life, following the commandments of God and walking from henceforth in His Holy ways?" You are to go forth from this table with new resolutions, new intentions; but a new dimension is added to these resolutions by the Lord's Supper. These resolutions are not made against a background of failure and futility. They're made against a background of faith and friendship with Jesus Christ.

Bill Hinson told about when his son was in Junior High. They were out in front of the parsonage one afternoon playing basketball. This father and son were having one of their better games, but the phone kept ringing. It was a girl who wanted to be the boy's steady girlfriend. Remember those going steady days in the seventh grade? And he'd go and talk for a moment and hang up; and she'd call back again. He was exasperated because Dad wanted to give him a couple of hours, and she kept interrupting. Finally, the conversation went sour, and he said, "Look, I don't want to be your boyfriend. I don't want to go steady with you."

When the girl said an ugly word, he said, "And that's another thing I don't like about you. You have a dirty mouth!"

She said, "John, don't you know everybody in our class talks like that but you?"

He said, "That's all right; my Daddy doesn't talk like that; and until I hear him talk like that, I'm not going to talk like that either."

As soon as Bill had a few moments, he found a private place of prayer, and he made a commitment to a son who by now has heard every kind of language there is. All he would have to do is see a current movie or two. Bill knew that, but he made a commitment that morning that even though he would hear all that, he'd never hear it from his Daddy. Friendship with Christ is like that.

One nature does feed on another, the weaker on the stronger, so that where one friend is perfect strength, we can think of all his weaker friends feeding on him. This is symbolized in the Holy Communion, for in communion with Jesus, our very souls feed on his nature as our bodies feed on bread. Resolutions can be kept for they're made against the background of faith and friendship with Christ. Here's another chance for new life—a time and a place for remembrance, reckoning and resolutions.

I came to my teacher with a quivering lip, my task undone.
"Master, give me another sheet, I have spoiled this one."
In place of the old sheet, stained and blotted,
He gave me a new one, clean, unspotted;
And into my glad face smiled,
"Do better next time, my child."

I went to the throne with a quivering heart, the old year done.

"Master, is there another chance for me? I have lost this one."

He took the old year, stained and blotted;
Gave me a new one, clean, unspotted;
Then down into my glad heart smiled,
"Do better next time, my child."

Valentine's Day
WANTED: A LOVING, LASTING MARRIAGE
Matthew 19:3-12, I Cor.13 (Esp. 4-5, 13)

A little while back, Ed Grisamore wrote a column for the Macon Telegraph about a funeral preached by my long-time friend, Earnest Veal. While Earnest was preaching the funeral of this couple, he said, "I want all of you to take note of what you're wearing today and with whom you're sitting. Remember everything you can about this day, for it's very likely that that there will never be another day in human history like it." He was burying a couple out from Wrightsville that had been married for 77 years and then died just a few hours apart on the same day. Paul said, "Nothing shall separate us from the love of God," but this couple seemed to be saying, "Nothing shall separate us from each other either." What a loving, lasting marriage!

When we hear about a marriage like that in our day, we're almost incredulous. It's a miracle isn't it? After all, we live in a culture where 40% of all American children can expect to experience the divorce of their parents, and where the shelf life of husbands, wives, and families is as disposable and perishable as a fresh container of milk. No wonder we marvel.

It's not that we've rejected marriage. Mae West used to say, "Marriage is a great institution. But I'm not ready for an institution yet." But that's not our society's problem. We've got 4 out of 5 people choosing to get married. But the 110 million+ married persons in the United States are asking the question, "How can I make my marriage last?" No young persons approaching the altar or even seeking out a justice of the peace are looking for failure. No couples in the midst of a marriage, whether it's their first or a later one, want that marriage shattered. Everybody who's seeking marriage or who's currently engaged in a marriage would be glad to sponsor the ad that is the title of this message, if they could be guaranteed what it's seeking. Wanted: A Loving, Lasting Marriage!

I wonder though how many would be willing to meet the qualifications that would fulfill the ad's requirements. I remember Senator Sam Nunn telling about the ad in the newspaper that read: Wanted: Man for Archeological Expedition – Must be 6 feet tall, a college graduate, and must have an adventurous spirit. A fellow came by and answered the ad, but the interviewer discovered that he was only 5 feet tall, hadn't even finished high school, and he said he was a coward. The interviewer said, "Well, why did you answer the ad?" The guy said, "Well, I just came by to tell you not to count on me."

If we want a loving, lasting marriage, there are certain qualifications that have to be met, and only those willing to measure up to the qualifications need apply. Jesus made this clear. If we get past his Scriptural divorce prohibition, it is always balanced with his giving anyone who's failed in life another chance, we hear him saying loud and clear, God is the marriage-maker. "What God has joined together, let no one put asunder." (Mt. 19:6) With this resounding praise of marriage and the uniquely elevated status that a husband and wife hold in God's plan of creation, we're not surprised that he said in Mt. 19:11-12, "Not everyone is mature enough to live a married life. It requires a certain aptitude and grace. - - -But if you're capable of growing into the largeness of marriage, do it." What are those aptitudes, what are those graces that would make us capable of growing into the largeness of marriage? If you ask, "How can I make my marriage last?" The answer is in the details. And who better than the Apostle Paul to give us some of those details in the 13th Chapter of I Corinthians:

Love never gives up.
Love cares more for others than for self.

Love doesn't want what it doesn't have.
Love doesn't strut,
Doesn't have a swelled head,
Doesn't force itself on others,
Isn't always "me first,"
Doesn't fly off the handle,
Doesn't keep score of the sins of others,
(NIV Keeps no record of wrongs,)
Doesn't revel when others grovel,
Takes pleasure in the flowering of truth,
Puts up with anything,
Trusts God always,
Always looks for the best,
Never looks back,
But keeps going to the end.

In other words, if you want a loving, lasting marriage, you have to be a good chemist. How many times have those of us who have counseled couples in trouble heard one of them say, "The chemistry just isn't there anymore." They say it like it's something that happens independent of them and their behavior. It's just a spontaneous chemical reaction of which we were the victims. But that phrase, "The chemistry just isn't there anymore," should be banished from our vocabulary. Each of us can maximize chemistry to make new chemical reactions happen. The chemistry wrong? Mix up some new chemicals. Stir up some different romance ingredients.

Now some do go at it wrong. Comedian Roger Dangerfield said, "We sleep in separate rooms, we have dinner apart, we take separate vacations---we're doing everything we can to keep our marriage together."

But when is the last time you left your spouse a love note, or even just said, "I love you?" Taken a stroll in the moonlight? Rubbed your mate's back? Given a 60-second hug? Sung a love song to your partner? Well, scratch that idea. Love and a lasting marriage is in the details, the chemical ingredients you put in. So plant a tree together, give a gift in honor of your marriage, renew marriage vows, buy the biggest wedding cake and invite friends over, exchange gifts you each would really appreciate. Just take her out to dinner, or bring it in? Chemistry between two people is responsive to mental and emotional processes over which we have tremendous control. That's right, you can make chemistry happen. If you don't feel the flutter in your heart for your spouse that you once did, if the magic is gone from your relationship, don't panic. You can change that. Paul put it; "Love never gives up. Love cares more for the other than for self. Love isn't always "Me first." He's talking about agape love, not just eros love. Not just passionate desire, but that passionate desire for the good of the other. Mix that in and see what kind of chemical reaction you get.

Off in a revival at Woodstock out visiting with the preacher, Harry Alderman, we went by the hospital so he could check on a member who had just given birth to a baby after a long, perilous incubation period. She'd been down for three months before birth, unable to do anything at home. The husband had to do his work and hers, and was getting over an accident himself. While we were in the room, a dozen roses arrived from the husband, and as she looked at the card, Harry thought about the husband's injury and said, "How's your husband?" She looked up and said, "Oh, he's wonderful!" She was smiling through tears of joy. Harry never did find out about the husband's health that day. But we both found out about the health of that marriage. That husband was a good chemist.

And Paul hints at the fact that if we want a loving, lasting marriage, we have to be bad mathematicians. He says, Love "Doesn't keep score of the sins of others." The NIV translates that, "Love keeps no record of wrongs." I was counseling a couple one time and the husband said, repeating the old saw we all have heard, "Every time we have a disagreement, she gets historical." He didn't say hysterical, he said historical. He said she remembered everything he had ever done wrong and could catalog it with date and time and place. She did a little of that in our session. They both needed to start keeping no record of wrongs. Paul said, love "Never looks back."

As important as it is to become a good chemist, it's equally important to become a bad mathematician. In marriage, each partner must be willing to put in more than he or she takes out. Psychiatrist Allen Fay said, "A patient once said to me, 'Marriage is a 50/50 proposition, isn't it?' I said, No, marriage is a 60/60 proposition. Each person has to do a lot more than what he thinks his share is." In a survey of 351 couples married for over 15 years, the ones who were happiest claimed that, "You have to be willing to put in more than you take out. Sometimes one member of the couple needs to give 90% while the other gives only 10%, as during a serious illness, job loss, or death in the family. A lasting marriage is one in which each partner "looks out for number two," not where each one is "looking out for number one."

Good math would tell you that in your relationship, if you had 10 loving, caring acts in your relationship bank, you ought to be able to withstand 10 terrible arguments. No! The researchers tell us that to be happy, couples have to have 10 to 20 times as much reserve of love and caring to help them through the rainy days in their relationship. One major argument can erase the effects of many positive interactions. Practice bad math. Boost your over all happiness by storing up far more acts of love and kindness than you'll ever need for balance. Being extravagant with your budget may tear you apart. But you can never be too extravagant with love. Practice some bad math.

But among the most critical requirements if you want a loving, lasting marriage is a good exercise program. Now, I'm not talking about our need for physical workouts as important as that is to ease the tension in marriages. I'm talking about what Paul points to when he says, "Love: Trusts God always, (and) "Always looks for the best." Among successful, long-lasting marriages, there is always an underlying given that both partners rely upon without hesitation. They flex the muscles of trust and bend the knees of prayer.

Trust may not seem glamorous or sexy, but many marriages have found out too late that without trust, there is nothing. Lack of trust is a cancer that rots away relationships. There was a woman who came to disbelieve her husband's faithfulness. She didn't trust him. She hired a private detective to follow him and report. After a week the detective came back and said, "I don't find anything out of the way, lady."
"Well, follow him another week."
At the end of another week he came back and said, "His behavior is without any reason for you to be suspicious."
"Follow him another week."
At the end of the third week, "Lady, you have no reason to distrust him."
"Follow him another week."
At the end of the fourth week he came back and said, "Lady, I don't find any grounds for your suspicion."
"Follow him another week, He's slick."

How many weeks? Now this calls for some arithmetic. How many weeks would he have to report to this woman that her husband was on good behavior for her to trust him? Do you know how many it would be? I'm going to give you the answer. It's forty eleven hundred weeks, or 846 years. Do you know why? Because trust is not what you do after you get a whole lot of proof.

Trust is giving. Trust is risk. Trust is open to the possibility of being hurt. Yes! Possibility of being wrong, yeah! But to the person who will not trust, final proof is never enough. For the person who will trust, and flex the muscles of trust, final proof is not necessary. That's why Paul says, "Love always looks for the best."

I counseled a couple in which the man mistrusted his wife almost to the point of having his wife followed. All I could do was ask her to recognize his weakness by always checking in with him when they were apart to quiet his mind's imaginings. He had had a failed marriage from infidelity. And I told him to flex the muscles of trust. Stop quizzing her. Stop checking on her. "Always look for the best." I've had a lot of failures in counseling, but the warmth with which they greeted me when I ran into them at a funeral 13 years later told me that something worked that time.

Does bending the knees of prayer help? Paul put it, "Love trusts God always." Jimmy Chester told me that he had a layman who said to him, "Jimmy, my wife literally saved my life." He said that for years they had had the habit of nightly devotionals. This couple got down on their knees and held hands across a chair before they got into bed. A recession came and he lost everything he had. With the recession came his deep depression and he planned to take his life the next day, had the gun and the spot picked out. But that night he said, "I heard my wife call my name before God in prayer." He said, "She literally saved my life."

Some here may have already experienced a loving marriage that was all too brief and you have to note that "It's not how long you make it, it's how you make it long." It's not the length, but the depth. It's not the quantity; it's the quality. You can rejoice in what you've known as you walk along the back roads of the rivers of your memory.

But others here may want to join me in responding to this ad, "Wanted: A Loving, Lasting Marriage." If so we need to practice some good chemistry, some bad math, and enter into an exercise program that flexes the muscles of trust and bends the knees of prayer.

If we do that, Ed Grisamore may not ever write about us in the Macon Telegraph, but we may experience "What God has joined together that no one can put asunder."

Passion/Palm Sunday
ABOUT FINDING MEANING
Mark 14:1-9

If there's anything that all of us really want it's that our lives would make sense. That our lives would somehow have meaning, that somehow we could make sense of what is happening to us in life. In Daniel Defoe's Robinson Crusoe, after being shipwrecked on a desert island, Crusoe finds himself about to go berserk. So he says, "After I had been there about Ten or Twelve Days, it came into my Thoughts, that I should lose my Reckoning of Time for want of Books and Pen and Ink, and should even forget the Sabbath Days from the working Days; but to prevent this I cut it with my Knife upon a large Post, in Capital Letters, and making it into a great Cross I set it up on the Shore where I first landed, viz. I came on Shore here on the 30th of Sept. 1659. Upon the Sides of this square Post I cut every Day a Notch with my Knife, and every seventh Notch was as long again as the rest, and every first Day of the Month as long again as that long one, and thus I kept my Kalander, or weekly, monthly, and yearly reckoning of Time." If he had not been able to make some sense of who and where he was, he would have gone crazy and would not have been able to survive.

Of all the tasks that a mother and a father have in a home, one of the chief tasks is this business of interpreting to the children the things that happen. A child wakes up in the middle of the night, "Mommy, Mommy, there's somebody out there!"

Then the mother carries the child to the window and looks out and says, "There's nothing out there. See, it was just the wind scrubbing a little limb against the screen." And the child settles down and goes to sleep.

The family dog dies… "Do dogs go to heaven, Daddy?" This is a question for Daddy. And of all the things that parents do, probably the business of interpreting what happens, some sort of sense and some sort of meaning to what happens, ranks above all other things that parents do. An uninterpreted life is unbearable.

Unexplained pain is unbearable. You go to the doctor and you say, "Doc, it starts about right down in here down in my lower back and I just can't sleep at night. Can you tell me what it is? I get up and I can't sleep and I get in my easy chair, and I still can't sleep. Uh, what do you think it might be?" If we could just know, we could stand it so much better.

If we have meaning, if we make sense of things, we can survive almost anything. We can survive even boredom. You take a housewife, a homemaker putting food in a dish to eat what's on the dish, to clean the dish, to put the dish up, to get it down again to put food on it. You make up the bed to get in the bed to make up the bed, and it's really not all that exciting. Being one of the few men in our society who can come in to lunch at home, if Day was still driving, I wouldn't be surprised if one day I found a note propped up against a tuna fish can that says, "Fix it yourself, I'm gone to the mall!" It's really not all that exciting. You mow the grass and water the grass and fertilize the grass so you can mow the grass and it just keeps coming back. We do all these things insensibly. We couldn't stand it; we couldn't bear this boredom if there weren't some sense in it... some meaning in it somewhere.

We squeeze meaning out of things that seem meaningless. I pulled for Cathy Cox for governor a few years back. I received this wonderful young woman into the Methodist Church back in Bainbridge when she was a senior in high school. I know her and love her and I truly believed that she'd make a great governor for the State of Georgia. But I know, and I think even Cathy knows, that there's the possibility of this scenario.

The campaign has been going on all year with vested energy from hundreds of workers and the family. And the election has been held and the reports from the vote have come in and they knew at nine o'clock that it was lost. But at 11 o'clock they come down the stairs at the grand ballroom to find the campaign workers still there trying with their silly hats to show some sort of enthusiasm. But they all know it was lost. The polls have already told the tale. But at 11 o'clock she comes down with her husband and faces all the workers and has to say, "I tell you, it doesn't really matter whether you win or lose. What matters in this campaign is your friendship." You just have to have some meaning when some things happen in life.

The Braves have lost seven out of nine at the start of the season, just can't seem to get it on track as they have in the past and the Manager has to face them. He comes in and says, "Maybe it was time that we had to be knocked off our pedestals a little bit, and learn that they're not going to just give it to us out there."

Now, what's he trying to do? He's trying to take the sweat and dirt from off the dressing room floor and mold it into meaning. They have to make some sense out of what's happening, so they can stand it. So they can sit around and say, "Well, we're down off our pedestals, so the only way is up, let's go!" But it has to be. We have to have it—this meaning.

The minister goes into the home; I did it back in Eastman, Georgia back in the sixties, early seventies. It makes me think about what some families with military children are going through now. The minister goes into the home and sees the picture of the young man in uniform on the table. And he says, "Your son?"

"Yes."

"Is he still in the service?"

And the man of the house says, "He's dead." And walks out into the back yard. Thrusts his hands down into his pockets like he would push the bottoms out of the pockets.

And the minister turns to the wife and says, "It's really hard for him, isn't it, after all this time?"

She said, "Yes, because his death in Viet Nam just made utterly no sense to him."

The minister says to her, "Well, how do you stand it?"

She said, "Well, I couldn't stand it if it didn't make some sense. I would go crazy." We all have to have it, to try to find some meaning, some purpose in the things that happen to us.

It's not only the things that happen to us but it's the things that we do. One of the things that can crush us is to go through life and suddenly discover that the things that I've done, the things that I do, nothing that I'm doing really makes any difference to anybody. You go to the party and they have these little triangular sandwiches and you nibble on them, because that's all there is, you know, and you drink the thimble-full of punch. And you make conversation—really heavy stuff. "You know it was nearly 90 degrees in Macon today. Really hot wasn't it? Right here in the middle of cherry blossom time! You didn't believe in global warming, but now you know it's coming." Really heavy stuff like that.

And then suddenly you realize that somebody has come into the room. And you look around and you see this lady making her way through, and people are greeting her. People are loving her. And you say, "Who is that?"

They say, "Why you don't know? That's Grace. Grace Thompson. You know she runs that program for the exceptional children. People call her Amazing Grace."

And you go, you speak to her, and you talk to her for about five minutes. Her face is aglow. She's full of life. She's full of radiance and joy some way or other. It's an engaged face, a concerned face.

And you go home that night and you try to purchase a little bit of sleep. And the only way you're able to purchase it is to say, "O God, sometime soon, somehow, I'm going to find some way that I can know that my life is meaningful. That it makes a difference to somebody." We just have to have it. We have to make sense out of life. We can't survive unless we do.

Our text today shows us that sometimes that difference that's made, that significance, that meaning, doesn't come to us until later. It's a sort of a gift of God on that that we said, or that that we did, or that that happened to us, that we don't know about at all at the time. And it comes as a kind of gift of God.

For here we have this woman that comes in from the street, in Mark's version of it, at the time of the anticipation of Christ's death. So far as we know, she was not aware of his upcoming death. But she comes and takes an alabaster jar of ointment and she breaks this costly nard over his head—this abundant fragrance. About 300 denarii's, about $60, and what might $60 have purchased in that day in ancient Israel? She just pours it over his head out of gratitude perhaps for something that he had done for her—a forgiveness that he had brought to her, a new direction in life. And in her extravagant love she just pours it out. And of course there was somebody there to criticize it. And they say, "Ah this could have been sold, and look at all the dried milk and diapers that we could have bought for this and really could have helped the poor." And they upbraid her.

And Jesus said, "Leave her alone, she's done a beautiful thing to me. I tell you what she's done. She's anointed my body for burial."

Now, they thought that what she did didn't make any sense at all. That fragrance would be dissipated in a moment, and gone, forgotten! She thought that she was just expressing her gratitude, her love for something he'd done for her. But Jesus said, "I tell you what she's done. She's anointed my body for burial. And wherever the gospel is preached, wherever the gospel is shed abroad this story will be told of her." And it has been, hasn't it?

She didn't know. You never know, really. She didn't know. But Christ took something that happened when she was just doing what she could, what she had available to her, and Christ took it and made it into a sacrament. "She has anointed my body for burial."

But I'm kind of glad that she didn't know in advance. If she had known she might have said, "Oh, oh, oh, "I'm anointing his body for burial." And she might have blubbered and cried and made a mess and spilled the nard all over the place. It was probably a good thing that she didn't know. As it was she did a simple act of gratitude and Christ took it and elevated it into the eternal and the profound.

So what am I after today? When I was taking homiletics in seminary, one of my teachers said that when you're preaching, you ought to always ask yourself before every sermon, "What are you trying to do to these people?" Or, "What are you trying to get these people to do?" So I ask myself, "Do I want my readers to set out to have a meaningful life?"

I don't know, I think that sometimes we try too hard to find meaning. We try to make things have meaning when they don't particularly have any meaning. I remember going to a youth retreat up in the mountains at Unicoi State Park, up on the Squirrels Nest. Some of you may have been up there. We had a bunch of young people trying to hang on to that mountain and keep from being washed away by some heavy summer rains, and in the midst of this, my Associate Pastor decided that we were going to have a meaningful worship service. We were going to have a communion breakfast. "Now we'll just have the eggs and grits and bacon and everything, but it's going to be just like communion."

And those young people came in there thinking, "Well, that's what it's supposed to be." So one of them came dressed up with a tie on—for breakfast at a camp! And they thought that we were supposed to have a meaningful service. And we tried to have a meaningful service. But what do you do with communion grits? What do you do with communion eggs? You just can't force meaning.

But I was with another group of young people about 38 strong up in the mountains one time and our bus broke down and we had to walk about 14 miles up and down that mountain with each other and save each other from falling off the mountain. We had to hitchhike rides for all thirty-eight of us, and would you believe a guy with a bus he'd converted into a family camper had room for all of us? So the youth group sang songs of gratitude to this family on the bus. When the thing was over, when it rained on our final dinner and we finally got on another bus on our way back home, there was not a single one of those young people who didn't say in their hearts, "You know, this has been more like church than church."

You never know. You never know when it's going to happen. You know what I think. I think that what we need to do is not to worry about whether things have meaning or not. Not try to force meaning into situations. But just do what we can. "She has done what she could." Just send that card. Send that letter. Just try to be appropriate to the moment you have before you. As the door opens for you to speak, speak. To give a little jar of perfume here, a cup of cold water here, a plate of warm food, a little boiled custard, make a phone call, put a little card in the mail. Go by the nursing home and say, "You didn't know I knew it was your birthday, did you?" Just the least little thing, whatever is appropriate for the moment. Put your ballot in the box. Just the least little thing. You don't know. Maybe. You don't know.

I suggest that we live simply, that we love generously, that we speak truthfully, that we serve faithfully, and just leave the rest to God. Just leave the rest to God. And you never know. Maybe someday he'll say to you, "I remember when I was hungry or naked or in prison and you came."

"Huh! I don't remember, I don't remember anything about you being... all I was doing was just trying to help out a little bit."

In the Bible, it's always the mark of the Saint, when she or he is surprised when told of the meaning of what they do. My Passion Sunday prayer for us all this day is that someday every one of us might be surprised by meaning. I think that's really all I wanted to say about finding meaning.

Ash Wednesday
FROM BROKEN HEART TO BRIGHT HOPE
Joel 2:1-17, Psalm 51:16-17, Matthew 26:27-28

One of the ongoing human problems that all religions of the world arose to deal with is the problem of sin or guilt, anxiety or angst. Some say that this is the greatest human problem and is the reason for the persistence of religious practice. The psychological self-help groups today, without purporting to be religious, nevertheless use a phrase that's one of my favorites. They call it, "stinking thinking"— negative thoughts that keep us from being healthy physically, mentally and emotionally. They come from the pocket of our personality called "low self-esteem."

"Stinking Thinking" includes thoughts like, "I've sinned, I'm stupid, and God has abandoned me or is punishing me." At some time in our life most of us have the feeling about ourselves that little Sam had. Two little boys, Ben and Sam, had been a pain in the neck to their mother. She was at the end of her patience, particularly with Sam, the older boy, who seemed to lead little Ben into all kinds of devilment. She demanded that Sam go down and talk to the preacher about their behavior.

The preacher must have been a Presbyterian because when Sam got in the office, he looked at him over his desk and asked him one of the questions out of the Catechism, the little book that some churches use to train kids in preparation for Church Membership. He said, "Where is God, Sam?" That's the first question in the book. "Where is God?"

Sam looked around the office, up on the bookshelves, out the window, and didn't see Him, so he didn't say anything.

Preacher said, "Where is God?"

Sam looked around again but didn't say anything.

Finally the preacher gave up and said, "Go home, Sam!"

So Sam ran home, up the stairs to his brother's room and said, "Ben, we're in big trouble. God's missing and they think we took Him!"

How do we get out of this big trouble we're in? The ancient Jews had a system of scapegoating. Here it is in Leviticus 16:21ff. "Aaron shall lay both his hands on the head of the live goat, and confess over it all the iniquities of the people of Israel, and all their transgressions, all their sins, putting them on the head of the goat, and sending it away into the wilderness." Later they sacrificed bulls and sheep and goats on the altar on the Day of Atonement to cleanse the people of their sins. They just killed those innocent animals and let their blood spill out on the altar thinking that that would appease their God.

The prophets came to understand that God really wasn't too keen on this blood sacrifice of animals and their thinking made it into the worship songs of the people like the 51st Psalm, verses 16-17:

"For you have no delight in sacrifice;
Were I to give a burnt offering, you would not be pleased.
The sacrifice acceptable to God is a broken spirit;
A broken and contrite heart, O God,
You will not despise."

The prophet Joel centers in on this theme in his recommendation to the people on how to escape their sin and guilt and its consequences. He says the answer is to, "Rend your hearts and not your clothing." Have you seen some of those news shots of people over in the Mid-East just tearing their clothing in religious services or protests? Over here we're much more civilized. We just tear our clothing on stage at the Super Bowl. Joel says," Don't go around tearing your clothes or trying to make outward blood offerings or burnt offerings.

Change your inner self." He says, "Rend your hearts and not your clothing."

He also says, "Return to the Lord your God." He thinks this is possible because of the nature of God. "For he is gracious and merciful, slow to anger, and abounding in steadfast love, and relents from punishing. Who knows whether he will not turn and relent and leave a blessing behind him, a grain offering and a drink offering?" In other words, our God is so loving and forgiving that instead of demanding you to leave sacrifices on the altar to sort of pay for your sins, God will reverse the process and pull a switch. If you come with a broken heart and a desire to leave your sins behind and inwardly change, God will be the one leaving a gift on the altar for you to help you get started in the new life again.

We might put it this way, that "God is like Francis Kim" or "Francis Kim is like God" in his dealing with sin and guilt. Francis Kim is owner of the Family Shoe Port in Honolulu. It's an athletic footwear store and a man was caught shoplifting. He stole a pair of shoes. Instead of having him put in jail, Francis Kim decided to forgive the 27 year-old man. He offered him a job, and drove him home from the police station! Mr. Kim said, "I don't think he would want to make a mess out of his life for one pair of shoes. He said he needed them, so I gave him a chance to earn them. If he went to jail it wouldn't do any good, he would just come out and steal more."

Police detective Mike Tanaka said, "We've had people drop charges before, but this is the first time I've had a complainant drop charges and hire the suspect just like that!"

The medieval Church designed Ash Wednesday and Lent to deal with the problem of sin, guilt, angst, stinking thinking. On the night that began Lent we were supposed to rend our hearts and not our garments. We were supposed to repent of our sins and turn away from them and enter into a forty-day period of Lent patterned after Christ's forty days in the wilderness in which we return unto the Lord. Maybe your church didn't observe an Ash Wednesday service, but that doesn't relieve us of trying to find some way to confess, repent, and receive pardon for our sins.

And, you know something? We can watch on Television from New Orleans the distortions and excesses of Fat Tuesday and Mardis Gras. That crude behavior is born out of the desire to have one last sinful fling before entering into this discipline of repentance and forgiveness in Lent. But gloating and pointing our fingers at the mistakes of others shouldn't keep us from finding some way to enter into this discipline for ourselves.

Fortunately, our Christ didn't leave us without a service and a way to do that all year long. When He instituted the Lord's Supper, he gave us such a service.

Matthew 26:27-28 "Then he took a cup, and after giving thanks he gave it to them, saying, 'Drink from it, all of you; for this is my blood of the new covenant, which is poured out for many for the forgiveness of sins.

If God is the kind of a God who drops the charges and hires the suspect just like that, we ought to confess our sins with some specificity. We need to come before Him with broken, contrite hearts counting on Him to put us back to work in His kingdom free from guilt. Dear reader: May that happen for you on this Ash Wednesday.

Good Friday
HIS EYE IS ON THE SPARROW
Luke 23:26-31, Acts 5:27-32

It was probably on Good Friday that some women who followed Jesus "bewailed and lamented" him, that is, out of their love and sorrow for his situation, they cried over him. They wept for him. At first glance it would seem that these women are doing a good and gracious thing. They are bewailing and lamenting the plight of this good man carrying his cross, bearing it to Golgotha. It seems a very natural thing to do. Certainly his plight was mournful. A good, innocent man was being falsely accused and put to death in the cruelest way that ancient civilization could devise. It would seem to be a touch of human pity that went a little way to redeem the desolateness of Jesus' last journey for us all. After all, don't people go to the Holy Land today and follow the steps of Jesus to the cross, which is called the Via Dolorosa, the way of tears? Don't we encourage people to re-enact the pity for him that was felt by these women on that journey?

Why then did Jesus say to them, "Do not weep for me?" Their pity met with a gentle rebuke, "Daughters of Jerusalem, don't weep for me!" Why did he say it?

The first answer is the obvious one provided by the biblical setting and attested to by all the biblical scholars. Jesus is predicting the fall of Jerusalem and the destruction of the temple that did come a little bit later in 70 A.D. He says, "Don't weep for me, but weep for yourselves and for your children. For the days are coming when you'll be glad you don't have any children. You wouldn't want them to undergo the violent destruction that comes when the Roman conquerors finally get fed up with this city. You surely don't want to be nursing any babies that'll just slow you down when you're trying to flee the city for your life. You'll be hunting cover to keep the babies in your arms from being dashed to the ground. You'll want the mountains to fall on you in preference to what will be happening to you when the end of the city comes. Motherhood will be a curse in those days instead of a blessing. So don't weep for me. Weep for yourselves and your children!"

Furthermore, he says, (vs. 31) "For if they do this when the wood is green, what will happen when it is dry?" This is the First Century way of saying, "You ain't seen nothing yet!" If fire can destroy living, green wood, it will certainly destroy the dry. Jesus is saying, "My fate, suffering even when I'm innocent, is certain to come to those who are not so innocent. If this can happen to an innocent man, what is going to happen to this whole wicked society? So don't weep for me. Weep for yourselves and your children. For you'll bear the brunt of the fallout from the super-destruction when it comes."

Why did Jesus say, "Don't weep for me, but for yourselves and your children?"

I think he said it because he's enunciating a principle that is apparent to those who are sensitive to it in all areas of life. So often when you have pity for a single individual undergoing the injustice or sorrow of events, it can defuse your concern to do something about changing yourself or your whole society. You can cry over the individual and forget about your own need for change to avoid that fate. You can cry over an individual and ignore the need for your whole town or culture or nation to change to avoid a worse fate.

Those women weeping for Jesus are like the alumni and officials of a great university a few years ago. They were lamenting, bewailing and bemoaning the fact that an innocent player was being blocked from doing the only thing in life that he knew how to do, that is, play football. It was all because of just a little grade discrepancy. After all, all the other schools were doing it. "You don't want us to have to play high school football at the college level, do you?" They were practically in tears over the matter, this poor kid that won't have a chance in life now. Not knowing at the time that they themselves were on the verge of massive monetary suits, loss of jobs, good names and reputations, and disqualification of the whole team to play because of duplicity. Don't weep for me, but for yourselves and your children.

Those women weeping for Jesus are like the young women's organization in the community I served that were distressed over the drug traffic and drug dependency of the youth in the schools even down to Junior High and grammar school age. They were thinking, "They're so young and so innocent that they are overly susceptible to the danger." But these young women didn't for a moment think about the pattern of alcohol use and abuse at their own parties. It didn't occur to them that the open swing set flirtations that were tolerated would soon lead to the dissolution and destruction of a dozen marriages and the children of those homes in that community. Don't weep for me, but for yourselves and your children!

One Saturday before Easter, the Atlanta Constitution carried a headline, "SPARROW, LAST ON EARTH, SINGS ITS SWAN SONG." Then followed a pitiful article telling about this one twelve-year-old, male Dusky Seaside Sparrow that was blind in one eye, living in a cage at Disney World Zoological Park. They were trying to get him to mate with a bird of another species since his species had gone from about 900 in the 60's down to this one last lonely sparrow. There's great sorrow in this article over the loss of this species and we feel pity for this one lonely old bird.

But I saw its picture in the paper and I heard the last single, mournful song he was singing. He sang, "Don't weep for me, but for yourselves and your children! Weep for yourselves when you allow the wetlands to be destroyed so that no wildlife can live. Weep for yourselves when you allow further condominium encroachment on beachhead and marshland and dunes so that your affluent children can have beer bashes on the eroding beaches before the hurricanes engulf the homes that have been built on what would have been the barriers. Don't weep for me when you cry, 'Give us the plants and the employment, but give the other states the toxic waste disposal!' It will all finally come home to roost. Not only will the birds have no roosting place, but you'll have no resting place or recreation place. Don't weep for me, but for yourselves and your children!"

Why did Jesus say, "Don't weep for me?" I think he had one more reason. The Acts reading gives us a clue. Acts 5:30-31, Peter said, "The God of our fathers raised Jesus whom you killed by hanging him on a tree. God exalted him at his right hand as leader and savior, to give repentance... and forgiveness of sins."

You see, through all his agony, Jesus believed it had a purpose. He had said it earlier, "And, I, if I be lifted up will draw all humankind unto me." He could foresee glorification of God, and his exaltation at his right hand for the purpose of causing repentance and forgiveness of sins for all. He knew that through his suffering and death there was hope, even for those gripped by patterns and practices for which they should be weeping for themselves.

So pity is not an appropriate response to the Christ. Repentance is! He didn't want pity for himself but repentance from them and from the whole city. He wanted a repentance, a changed life that begins with a sorrow, a weeping for the self and society that is sometimes the head and font and beginning of true repentance. Only in this way can forgiveness and the new life begin. "So don't weep for me, but for yourselves and your children. Let your look at my road to that cross put you on your road to repentance, because at the end of that road you'll find me alive to walk with you forever."

It may be too late for the dusky seaside sparrow. I never did hear whether that belated breeding experiment worked or not. But Jesus said, "Are not five sparrows sold for two pennies and not one of them is forgotten before God? Why even the hairs of your head are all numbered." Notice he said the hairs of your head, not the hairs of my head. Maybe that explains something. But he says, "Fear not; you are of more value than many sparrows." It may be too late for the dusky seaside sparrow, but because of Jesus' death and resurrection and the repentance and forgiveness he offers, Praise God! It's not too late for us! That's the good news! "His eye is on the sparrow, and I know he watches me!"

Do you remember the work, The Great Hunger, by Johan Bojer? Do you remember the principal character, Peer Holm, who was a famous engineer? He had built bridges to span the mighty rivers. He had laid railroads across the desert, tunnels beneath the streams. He was gifted in so many areas. While still a rather young man, the situation reversed. He lost his health, and consequently his standing. The one who had appeared before kings and rulers was carried on a toboggan of ill fortune back to his old village to be a blacksmith's helper and to till the soil around that little town.

People couldn't believe it, the great Peer Holm reduced to that. If you remember the story, you know that he lived beside a neighbor who had a vicious dog. Peer Holm was afraid for his little girl, his only child. He said to that man, "Could you chain up your dog?"
And the man said to Peer Holm, "Keep your mouth shut, pauper!"

One day, that which Peer Holm had feared the most came to be a reality. He was coming back from the field, heard the scream of his little girl, ran and tore that vicious animal away from her throat, but it was too late. The life was gone from her little body. The people pitied poor Peer Holm. The sheriff shot the dog, and the villagers wanted to run that neighbor out of town, but they didn't. They just shunned him; they ostracized him. And in the spring when he plowed his field, they wouldn't sell him any seed. His field was left bare. The boys hooted at him on the street.

One moonlit night, Peer Holm could stand it no longer. He got up and took a half-bushel of his own grain, and went over and sowed it in the field of his neighbor. You can't keep something like that a secret. Later in the spring, the villagers saw a bare spot in Peer Holm's field, and they saw grain growing in his neighbor's field. They came to Peer Holm and said, "You, of all people! Why did you do it?"

Peer Holm said, "I did it in order that God might exist in our community."

Some who didn't understand continued to pity poor Peer Holm and hate the neighbor. But some were brought to repentance and forgiveness as the message from the road to the cross was heard clearly in the town. "Don't weep for me, but for yourselves and your children." Maybe today, if we begin to weep even a little bit for ourselves, and our children, and our town, and our society, and our nation, and our world—maybe we can learn to walk the road of repentance and forgiveness with the resurrected Jesus.

❖

Easter Day
AHEAD OF ME TO GALILEE
Genesis 31:19-21, 32c-35, Matthew 28:1-10

Are you surprised by the focus of the message of the angel and the message of Jesus on resurrection morning? The Angel says just two things to the women: "Go quickly and tell his disciples,
1. 'He has been raised from the dead, and
2. indeed he is going ahead of you to Galilee; there you will see him.'
This is my message for you." Then after telling the women not to be afraid, Jesus just boils it down to one message: "Go tell my brothers, (i.e. disciples), to go to Galilee; there they will see me." Why go to Galilee to see the resurrected Christ?

Wouldn't there have been a better chance to see him if you just hung around the tomb? For many people, that's all the resurrection story is about. It's about life after death in the hereafter for loved ones. And to be sure, that's a legitimate by-product of the resurrection. John has Jesus assuring us, "If I go and prepare a place for you, I will come again and receive you unto myself, that where I am there you may be also." So we give our memorial Easter Lilies, and windows and pews in the church, and we never forget our loved ones, and we rejoice that's he's the conqueror of death. We can never minimize that.

But we have to remember that when the women were charged with the message of Easter, "they left the tomb quickly with fear and great joy," and ran to tell his disciples to, "go to Galilee."
It was on their way from the tomb where, "Suddenly Jesus met them and said, "Greetings!" If we see him beyond the grave, he has to greet us in Galilee first. If we experience him in the hereafter, we have to find him in the here first. We meet the risen Christ not at the grave only, but in Galilee.

I'm a little surprised that they weren't charged with telling them to go to Jerusalem if they wanted to see the risen Jesus. If I had been running the production, that's where I would have had him to appear. The first thing I would have had him to do would have been to put that fox, Herod, and the High Priest, and Pilate "in their place." Wouldn't that have been gratifying? All of us who believe in the resurrection so desperately want the rest of the world to believe it, and this would have been the ideal place, Jerusalem, where he'd been unjustly tried and condemned.

Why not flaunt his resurrected body before the soldiers who had mocked him and seen him die? We so desperately want proof. In the post-resurrection documents which were not allowed in the canon of New Testament Scripture, they would have the risen Christ appear in public, on the street—going into Wal-Mart, and the Mall and City Hall and the Civic Center and everywhere, just scaring people. "Isn't that Jesus?"

"That's Jesus!" Because the church wanted so much for everybody to believe it—just wanted to prove it.

But our Bible won't have it. It knows that faith dies from proofs, just as true love perishes when it demands proofs of another's love. Peter in Acts 10:40-41—"But God raised him on the third day and allowed him to appear, (Now note this.), not to all the people, but to us who were chosen by God as witnesses, and who ate and drank with him after he rose from the dead." This verse summarizes the point made by all the resurrection narratives—Jesus appeared only to believers.

In an old Upper Room publication I picked this up:
· "Only the friends of Jesus saw him.
· The resurrected Christ never appeared to his enemies, but only to those who loved him.

·   He didn't confront Caiaphas and say to him and his colleagues, 'Here I am alive again, hale and hearty, ready to cleanse the temple again.'

·   He never appeared to Pilate in his judgment hall with the words, "Pilate, you failed. You thought you had killed me. But I'm alive, more alive than ever. And I'm starting again today in a bigger way."

·   To Pilate and Caiaphas and all the unbelieving multitude, Jesus was dead—and he remained dead.

BUT to those who loved him, whose souls were attuned to his, he appeared in the garden of Joseph, on the road to Emmaus, in the Upper Room, beside the Sea of Galilee, on the crest of Olivet.

·   SO IT IS TODAY—You won't see Christ at this Easter-time unless you love him."

And the place to go to see him is Galilee. He said so himself, "Tell my disciples to go to Galilee; there they will see me." But where's Galilee for us? Wasn't Galilee for the disciples the place where they had worked, some of them in the common trade of fishermen? Wasn't that the place he had called them and taught them—the everyday world? And isn't that where we're going to see the resurrected Christ if we're ever to see him? In fact, the angel's language suggests that no matter where we go in our ordinary world the risen Christ will be there ahead of us—"indeed, he is going ahead of you to Galilee." AHEAD OF ME TO GALILEE!

We who have followed this faith for years shouldn't be surprised. Really the point of the unusual story from Genesis is just this. When Jacob worked for fourteen years for his wife Rachel and finally took her away from the home of her father Laban, Rachel stole her father's household gods. When she left her ancestral home she wanted to take her gods with her. She even hides them under a camel's saddle, sits on them, and won't rise up to greet her father as she pretends to be in her period. She does this so they won't be found and taken away from her. She couldn't think about traveling to a new land with the man she had married without taking along these petty little gods.

Little did she know that she had married a man whose God never had to be carried along as a part of the baggage, but a God who would always go before them and be where they could never go beyond his guidance and judgment and love and care. Little did she know that she would have a share in the ancestry of the one who would send the message through the women to the disciples that he was going before them into Galilee.

I love the story of the little girl who was told that the family was going to have to leave Georgia and move to Alabama. She loved her church and Sunday School and her home so much, so the parents were especially concerned as they knelt with her by her bed to say her prayers the night before they were to move. She blessed Mommy and blessed Daddy, and then for a final word she said, "Goodbye, God, we're moving to Alabama."

Don't believe it. God is not just with us in the comfortable, familiar places and stages of our lives. Even when you have to leave the old church and you've lost some family members, and you go through the traumatic experience of a new school or seeking new work in new places, the angel says, "he is going ahead of you to Galilee, there you will see him." Ahead of me to Galilee!

Paul found it to be true. When I had to teach a Sunday School class once, the lesson was on the resurrection, and I told that group that though I agreed with 99 and 44/100% of the writer's lesson, I had to reject outright one statement he made. He said, "Because of Christ's Ascension, his post-resurrection appearances have ended." Try telling that to Paul. Paul based his claim to being an apostle on just such a post-resurrection appearance that occurred after Christ's Ascension. (I Cor. 15:7) He says, "He appeared to James, then to all the apostles. Last of all... he appeared also to me." And he goes on to say, "his grace toward me has not been in vain." He ranks this "after ascension" appearance as just as valid as any of the others. And what was that appearance of the risen Christ like for Paul?

He was on the road to Damascus to persecute the Christians there. Read the whole thing in Acts 22:6-21, but suffice it to say here that the risen Christ spoke to him, "Saul, Saul, why are you persecuting me?"

Paul says, "Now those who were with me saw the light but did not hear the voice of the one who was speaking to me. I asked, 'What am I to do, Lord?' The Lord said to me, 'Get up and go to Damascus. There you will be told everything that has been assigned to you to do.'"

Go to Damascus? Why that was where Paul was already headed. I don't think that it's any accident that the 140 miles from Jerusalem to Damascus went through Galilee. That had given Paul a chance to think about all that he had heard that Jesus taught, all that he said and did while he was in Galilee. Yes, it was still "Go to Damascus." But what a difference!

Jesus says, "Rise, go into the city, and you will be told what to do." Up to this moment Paul had been doing what he liked, what he thought best, what his will dictated. After the risen Christ appears we are told what to do. There's a new center to our being. Never again would he take his way, but ever after Jesus' way. Now we call him not, Saul, but Saint Paul. A saint is just a sinner—revised and edited by the risen Christ. Oh don't we long for this experience for ourselves and for our world?

There's a Country and Western Song entitled "Somebody Paints the Wall." The refrain goes, "Whenever I make my mark—somebody paints the wall." Anybody not know what that means? But it made me think about the pathetic people who go around our cities now painting meaningless graffiti on the walls downtown. My former members, Ronnie and Marcia Thompson, who run Mrs. Wilkes Boarding House, had the front wall of their home in Historic Savannah all painted up with graffiti by somebody. They had to go out and repaint their front wall. Don't these people know that as long as they are self-centered, seeking to make some mark of attention for themselves that somebody's always going to come along and paint the wall? Oh that they and we could go to Galilee!

And even people on the dastardly road to Damascus have met the risen Jesus. I heard Gene Smith, a Gideon Speaker, tell about a life of profligacy and waste in which he had misused people all over Georgia. After his conversion he remembered a fellow in McDonough to whom he had given a bad check for $30. At the time, he figured up the interest and the number of years and it came to $67. He went by his store and paid a shocked storekeeper. He said, "The man didn't even remember it, but I did, and I had to make it good." He saw the risen Christ on the road to McDonough.

> On the road to Emmaus,
> On the road to Damascus,
> On the road to McDonough,
> On the road to Macon?

Thank God on this resurrection morning that he's gone ahead of me to Galilee.

❖

Mother's Day/Christian Home Sunday
HOME AND THE WELLNESS ISSUE
II Kings 4:8-37, III John 1-8, 13-15

A little girl forgot the lines she was to speak in a church pageant. Her anguished mother on the front pew gestured and silently formed the words with her lips, but to no avail. Finally, in desperation the mother whispered the cue: "I am the light of the world."

Instantly the little girl's face relaxed and with supreme confidence she began in a loud voice: "My mother is the light of the world!" Many of us who are at worship here today could join with that little girl in saying that our mothers were or are the light of the world.

But we wouldn't focus just on motherhood today. This is a day when the church traditionally focuses on the Christian home. In order to do that this morning I want us use this story of the prophet Elisha and the Shunammite Woman. This woman had been hospitable to the itinerant man of God providing him with a bed, a chair, a table and a lamp whenever he passed her way. In return, Elisha had blessed her and her husband so that they might have a son. But the child falls critically ill and the mother makes a trip to Mount Carmel to seek Elisha's help in healing him. He later responds with the miracle in which he raises the Shunammite woman's child. But our text today comes as a prelude to that miracle that restores the health of that ancient home. It comes at the point where she has come to seek his help.

When the man of God saw her coming, he said to Gehazi his servant, "Look, yonder is the Shunammite; run at once to meet her, and say to her, 'Is it well with you? Is it well with your husband? Is it well with the child?'"

And she answered, "It is well."

Here are questions from the 9th century before Christ posed by the prophet Elisha: Is it well with you? Is it well with your husband? Is it well with the child? But these questions are timeless. They strike at the core of the wellness of our whole society in any era. This is true because if the home is well, our whole life has a chance to be well. But if the home is sick, there is the shaking of the foundations.

Old Russian peasant log houses were constructed around a key log running under the center of the floor and sticking out the end. To pull the house down, a tractor simply had to jerk back and forth on this key log until the entire structure collapsed. The Russian word used for shaking the key log is also the word for agitation. It means, "to shake to pieces from underneath." A case can be made that our culture is shaking to pieces because of the agitation and disintegration of the key log, the home.

We can toss off the statistics: Half of all marriages end in divorce. Seventy-five percent of all divorces involve children. Is there a problem with that? Here's the poem of a ten-year-old latchkey child being treated for depression:

Divorce shakes you off the ground.
Divorce whirls you all around.
Divorce makes you all confused.
Divorce forces you to choose.
Divorce makes you feel all-sad.
Divorce pushes you to be mad.
Divorce makes you wonder who cares.
Divorce leaves you thoroughly scared.
Divorce makes a silent home.
Divorce leaves you all alone.
Divorce is supposed to be the answer.
Divorce, in fact, is emotional cancer.

This is not to condemn those who have tried so hard to make it work, but have recognized the reality that sometimes there is more sadness, and madness, and silence, and scaredness in homes that are tombs of abuse and abandonment, or even just simple neglect. Like the scene from the movie, The Doctor—This cynical, successful heart surgeon has his life attitude turned around by his own bout with cancer. And when he comes home unexpectedly in the middle of the day to do something he has never done before—to be with his family, his wife calls to their young son playing outside. She says, "Come in and say hello to your father."

The boy races into the room without even noticing his father standing at the other end. He picks up the phone automatically, "Hi, Dad. Hello, hello."

Then turning to his mother he says, "Well, Mom, we must have got cut off."

The parents in Chicago who faced charges because they left two small children home alone, apparently on purpose as they took a vacation to Mexico, were not divorced.

Why is it that in this country with one of the highest murder rates in the world, one and a half times as many Americans kill themselves as are killed by others? In a recent year (2005) over 32,000 Americans committed suicide. On the average day 90 Americans kill themselves, 14 of them under 25, five under 20. According to research scholars cited in The *Enigma of Suicide*, the primary underlying cause of the rising suicide rate among American youth is the breakdown in the family and the consequent loss of a sense of self-worth. (Colt, 41-42)

All homes: together, divorced, single parent, foster-parent, and adoptive-parent need to hear this:

Today I said, "Clean your room right now!" I failed to say, "Thanks for doing a neat job."

Today I said, "Hurry up. You're late!" I failed to say, "I enjoy having you around."

Today I said, "How in the world did you tear your jeans?" I failed to say, "You're more important than things to me."

Today I said, "Look at this mess!" I failed to say, "I like the way you share with friends."

Today I said, "Don't talk so loud!" I failed to say, "Your ideas are important to me."

Today I said, "Don't forget to empty the trash!" I failed to say, "You accept responsibility well."

Today I said, "I wish you'd stop that silly giggling!" I failed to say, "I'm glad you're so happy today."

Today I said, "Have you finished your homework?" I failed to say, "I'm glad you do your best!"

Today I said, "I'm too busy!" I failed to say, "Let's do something together."

Today I said, "I need some peace and quiet!" I failed to say, "I'm glad you're my child."

Today I said, "Don't you ever do that again!" I failed to say, "I love you." (Blevins, Living With Children, 43-44)

Real parents and grandparents are people who carry photographs where their money used to be.

Is it well with you? Is it well with the child? What would a home be like if it could answer this question positively? What would be the nature of the family if it were to be the key log that holds our culture together? Some clues are found in John's letter to Gaius, a part of which was given for your reading. In his estimation it's obviously a healthy home. Did you catch it?

John says to Gaius, "I pray that all may go well with you and that you may be in good health, just as it is well with your soul."

He knows that it's well with the family's soul so all he has to pray for is that the rest of the family's life will stay in harmony with that. The roots of this wellness are several:

That house is like a church where everybody is known by name. "Greet the friends there each by name." It makes me think about the old story of the preacher calling on a large farm family for the first time and noting that the house was just full of children. He was amazed. He said to the mother. "How many children do you have?"

She said, "Let me see. There's Joe and John and Ellie, and Alice, and..."

He stopped her. He said, "Oh, I didn't mean you had to name them all. I just wanted to know the number."

She said, "They have names, not numbers!"

I don't think it's any accident that this letter says, "I hope to see you soon, and we will talk together face to face." This was a house where names were known and face to face talking went on. Susan Jacoby remembers, "The summer hours before twilight, when I'd follow my father out to his backyard garden and talk to him until my mother called us in for supper. I never heard him say, 'Leave me alone.'"

And this was a house known for its hospitality. I saw a sign in a store window. It said, "Half-price sale on Welcome Mats." Maybe that's part of the problem today. Not enough homes display welcome mats. But John points out that this is a characteristic of Gaius' home when he says, "Beloved, you do faithfully whatever you do for the friends, even though they are strangers to you; they have testified to your love before the church."

Here's a home that's generous to itinerant church workers, sending them on their way after food, conversation, bed, breakfast and support.

You don't believe such a spirit has an impact on the children who live in that house! I remember a tenant farmer family with five children. The father was the lay-leader in the most country of my five country churches on that circuit. Day and I thought they couldn't afford it, but they'd have us come eat with them after church. He'd look at that table full of simple Southern cooking with my four and his seven gathered round it, and with a twinkle in his eye he'd say, "Now you see what it is. If you're a mind to eat it up from me and the chillun', just take out and help yourself."

I wasn't surprised in later years to discover that the little 11- year- old daughter who played the piano for the Worship services at their church became the editor for the magazine "*Engage-Social Action*" for the Board of Church and Society for the entire United Methodist Church. In a letter at Christmas she told how she and her husband with their church had just finished building their 4th house for Habitat for Humanity. It's not an accident that generous hospitality is at the heart of the home of the Shunammite woman and the home of Gaius the Elder.

The wellness was evident on another count. John says, "I have no greater joy than this, to hear that my children are walking in the truth." What truth was that? It's that truth referred to when Jesus said, "I am the way the truth and the life." This home was focused outside itself, on a higher, nobler truth than just its own self-interest. In that home, greater than the joy of being financially successful, greater than the joy even of knowing that your children were quote, "Successful," was the joy of knowing that they were devoted to something and someone outside themselves—bigger than the self.

You probably attend a church that was built with contributions by many people that had no blood children that could benefit from it, but that sense of the larger Christian family was still there. It's like old man Des Tuttle put it to me one time while we were watching construction on his church. I knew he had watched every beam and nail and brick go into that structure. I said, "Des, why are you so interested in this building? You don't have any children, do you?"

He said, ""No, but somebody put a church here for me, and we pay our debt to the past by obligating ourselves for the future." You see without blood family, he could still say, "I have no greater joy than this, to hear that my children are walking in the truth."

One of the biggest failures of our families is the notion that the home exists only for the personal fulfillment of its members. When Dan Coats sat on the Senate Committee that deals with children and families he said, "Many parents, obsessed with their own fulfillment have lost the values of sacrifice and commitment. The family for them is no longer a 'we' and a launching pad to send out servants for our whole society, but it becomes an exercise in mutual therapy for the self-centered egos of its members. If any of the members, parent or child, finds that the therapy is insufficient, they're free to leave!" (And they often do whether or not any of the crises being faced are real.) How different is the home of which it is said, "It is well with your soul." That kind of home can withstand the worst that the world can throw at it.

In 1873, Chicago lawyer Horatio G. Spafford sent his wife and four daughters on a European trip, with plans to join them later. His family sailed on the SS Ville du Havre that was struck by another ship and sank. Hearing of the tragedy he had cabled ahead to her destination. "Are you well? Are the girls well?"

When Mrs. Spafford reached Cardiff, Wales, she cabled her husband: "Saved alone." She had survived but the daughters were washed overboard.

Spafford sailed to meet his wife and somewhere near the scene of the shipwreck where they lost their four daughters he wrote the words of that great hymn:

> When peace like a river attendeth my way,
> When sorrows like sea billows roll,
> Whatever my lot, thou hast taught me to say,
> "It is well, it is well with my soul!"

As we think about HOME AND THE WELLNESS ISSUE, can we respond to the Word of God by saying, "It is well with my soul?"

Baccalaureate Sunday
IF I WERE YOUNG AGAIN
Romans 12:1-12a
J B Phillips Modern English

With eyes wide open to the mercies of God, I beg you, my brothers and sisters, as an act of intelligent worship, to give him your bodies, as a living sacrifice, consecrated to him and acceptable by him. Don't let the world around you squeeze you into its own mold, but let God re-mold your minds from within, so that you may prove in practice that the plan of God for you is good, meets all his demands and moves towards the goal of true maturity.

As your spiritual teacher I give this piece of advice to each one of you. Don't cherish exaggerated ideas of yourself or your importance, but try to have a sane estimate of your capabilities by the light of the faith that God has given to you all. For just as you have many members in one physical body and those members differ in their functions, so we, though many in number, compose one body in Christ and are all members of one another. Through the grace of God we have different gifts. If our gift is preaching, let us preach to the limit of our vision. If it is serving others let us concentrate on our service; if it is teaching let us give all we have to our teaching; and if our gift be the stimulating of the faith of others let us set ourselves to it. Let the one who is called to give, give freely; let the one who wields authority think responsibly; and let the one who feels sympathy for others act cheerfully.

Let us have no imitation Christian love. Let us have a genuine break with evil and a real devotion to good. Let us have real warm affection for one another as between brothers and sisters, and a willingness to let others have the credit. Let us not allow slackness to spoil our work and let us keep the fires of the spirit burning, as we do our work for God. Base your happiness on your hope in Christ.

IF I WERE YOUNG AGAIN 55

"If I Were Young Again." Have you thought about that? The form for our thought on this subject is suggested not only by the Scripture, but also by an incident from the life of the late Sir Winston Churchill. In his writings, Sir Winston would quite often end sentences with prepositions. This was a violation of the English grammar of his time called a dangling preposition. Once he received a critical letter from a lady who was an English grammar purist. She belabored him for setting such a bad example when he was acknowledged as a literary genius. She said it was beneath her and should be beneath him to ever end a sentence with a preposition. He wrote her back and said, "Madam, that is the sort of intellectual snobbery up with which I will not put." That's the sort of sentence up with which you will wind if you don't end sentences with prepositions sometimes.

So I want to dangle some prepositions in front of you as I tell you what I would do if I were young again. Maybe the dangling preposition will help these things to stick in your minds and hearts and lives.

First of all, I would try to be sure I had a self fit to live with. Edgar Guest penned a poem to say,

> I have to live with myself, and so
> I want to be fit for myself to know.
> I want to be able as days go by,
> Always to look myself straight in the eye.
> I don't want to stand with the setting sun
> And hate myself for the things I've done.

This is a demand for integrity and honesty with others and with the self. But a college girl from the university of Georgia stopped Bishop Arthur J. Moore on the steps of First Methodist Church in Athens after he had preached on the Ten

Commandments. She said with tongue in cheek, "Bishop, I know what the 11th commandment is."

He said, "What is it?"

She said, "Don't get caught!"

Seventy percent of Public High School students admit to serious test cheating in anonymous surveys. It would be hard to understate technology's role in the current wave of cheating. Students flock to online term-paper mills that sell reports on virtually any topic -- often with bibliographies and appropriate formatting. They use camera phones to send and transmit pictures of tests. Their MP3 players can hold digitized notes. Their graphing calculators can store formulas necessary to solve math problems.

Who can live with the self when this is a part of life... when you have to sneak and hide and cover up through life? The great Phillips Brooks put it like this, "To keep clear of concealment, to keep clear of the need of concealment, to do nothing which you might not do out on the middle of the Boston Common at noonday... I cannot say how more and more that seems to me to be the glory of a young life. It is an awful hour when the first necessity of hiding anything comes. The whole life is different thenceforth. When there are questions to be feared and eyes to be avoided and subjects which must not be touched, then the bloom of life is gone. Put off that day as long as possible. Put it off forever if you can."

But how do you do this? Shakespeare on the lips of Hamlet has a word for us, "To thine own self be true, and it must follow as the night the day, Thou canst not then be false to any man." But to what self is it that you are true? Isn't it the God-given self? Our faith tells us that we are created in the image of God. Shouldn't we try to find and be true to that God-given self?

I have noticed that through our teenage years we try on different selves like a young woman might go into a store and try on different dresses to see if she likes them. This is a natural thing and fairly harmless in the early teenage years. A girl decides that she's going to be the popular type with a bright, witty word for everybody... the big mixer with a string of boyfriends. But finds she can't pull that off so she decides that she'll be the "I don't care" type... no dates, no popularity, so she'll wear the mask "I don't care." This doesn't have enough distinction so she tries being the intellectual type. She goes around with horn-rimmed glasses and a great bundle of books under her arm and coolly shows her detachment from all these trivial things the other students bother with.

Or a boy might decide that he'll be the Big Man On Campus, head of every organization, at the center of every extra-curricular. Or he might try to be the football hero, the strong silent type. So with bulging biceps and a "nope" and a "yep" for the range of his conversation, he picks his way pigeon-toed across the campus.

But as older youth, you should have begun to find yourself, the self that you really are. Our Scripture put it, "Don't cherish exaggerated ideas of yourself or your importance, but try to have a sane estimate of your capabilities by the light of the faith that God has given to you all." Find out who it is that God intends for you to be and be it. As an old "Mammy" put it to her charges, "Be what you is, not what you ain't, cause when you is what you ain't, you ain't what you is."

If I were young again, I would try to be sure I had a self fit to live with.

Another proposition preposition I want to dangle in front of you is this... I would try to find a work fit to work at. Watching a game show one night on TV, I noted a guest on the show who was billed as a direct descendent of Vasco Da Gama, the great explorer and adventurer who found the first water route to the far East. When it was revealed what his occupation was it was noted that he repaired pool tables for beer halls. A heritage of adventure and exploration had wound up at a dull, dead-end street of beer bottles and billiards.

This can happen to anyone who goes out into life letting chance determine occupation. There are those who just let Uncle Sam worry about what they'll wind up doing. There are those who dully resign themselves to just four or five things at the most that they might possibly be and do. They limit themselves. Michael Phelps, who won a record eight Gold medals in swimming at the Summer Olympics in China, said, "You can't put a limit on anything. The more you dream, the farther you get."

Most high school graduates go out into life with limits on their dreams when the Library of Congress lists over 30,000 different occupations in this country. The Encyclopedia of Occupations lists over 1500 gainful employments, and we know that 85% of the people in this country work at 250 of these. There's a world of work out there and so many fields of service are just crying for people to take them up. The needs of this world are tremendous and people have talents to meet those needs. One of our rural workers in the United Methodist Church said, "Your vocation is found where your talents and abilities meet the needs of the world." It's terrible to waste food when people are hungry and it's terrible to waste cloth when people are cold. But it's more terrible to waste a life when there's so much that needs doing in our world.

Another factor you have to take into account if you're to find a work fit to work at is the revolution in cybernetics and automation. I walked through the peanut butter plant over at Dawson, Georgia and was impressed with the number of rote jobs that I still saw in operation. Even my inexperienced eye could count ten jobs that would soon be replaced by a machine. If we're to be able to continue to work in a generation like this, we must be above all things retrainable. We must equip ourselves with the basics in understanding and education so that we can turn in new directions when our economy and automation demand it. Only by constant learning and retraining can we do as our Scripture says… "Keep the fires of the spirit burning as we do our work for the Lord." If I were young again, I would try to always keep myself fit to work and find a work fit to work at.

Then, if I were young again, I would keep a love fit to wait for. Now you know the area that I'm about to talk about. Somebody said that life is one thing after another, but love is two things after each other. It's not long before we become aware of this area of life. A boy just out of grammar school coming into Junior High saw a pretty little blond walk down the hall. He said to his buddy, "Boy, when I quit hatin' girls, she's the one I'm gon' quit hatin' first."

A boy said to a senior, "Bill, has she kissed you yet?"

He said, "No, but she's steamed my glasses twice."

It's become somewhat popular to think that the ancient commandments and taboos against sex before marriage are out-dated and that there are no hard consequences. Talk about "the new morality" has made some forget the chaos and almost irreparable damage that can come from irresponsible love. There's a passage in Kierkegaard in which the brokenhearted victim of a promiscuous love affair writes to her seducer, her former love. She writes,

"John, I do not say, 'My John.' That I now see you never were. I am heavily punished for ever letting such an idea be my joy. Yet… yet mine you are… my seducer, my deceiver, my enemy, my murderer, the spring of my calamity, the grave of my joy, the abyss of my misery. I call you mine and I am thine… thy curse forever. Oh do not think that I will put a dagger into you and slay you. But flee where you will, I am yours to the earth's ends... yours. I am yours in your last hour. Yours, yours, yours... your curse."

Now no young man or woman who envisions a life of oneness with a beloved in marriage wants to be shackled with a thing like that. When relations like this go on, no matter how prevalent they are, they make marks that never heal and they mar future relationships of love and trust and commitment and responsibility.

On a test in a college the students were asked, "What is sex for?" The majority answers were, "Having Children" and "Having Fun." Now, though there is great pleasure in sex, and though it is the way that God has provided for replenishing the race, our faith has a larger much more beautiful answer than this. What is sex for?

·It's the most personal way for one person to say to another person, "I am yours, only yours, forever." God who made a unique you and a unique me unites us into one through this act.

·Sex is the very personal way two people are fulfilling the needs of each other for love.

·In sex we find the deepest meaning of really knowing another person in tenderness and understanding, commitment, trust and responsibility. The Bible catches this when it says, "Adam knew his wife Eve."

·This is the sacred method God has given for the creating of life, for reproduction. But since we are made in the image of God, a man and woman who enter into this act are cooperating in the reproduction of the image of God in the earth.

What a marvelous, sacred beautiful gift God has made to us in sex. If other beautiful gifts are given to us, our inclination is to take care of them. No school kid would think of destroying her cell phone. No student would tear up his laptop, I-pod, iPad or game-boy if he was given one. How much more should we guard and keep one of the priceless gifts of life.

Once Jesus prayed for his disciples who would come after him and he said, "Father, for their sakes I sanctify myself." If I were young again, I would think about the girl or boy I was to marry, whether or not we had met yet. I would think about the little girl I might one day have and the kind of young woman I would want her to be. I would think about the boy whom God might give me and the kind of young man I would want him to be, and I too would pray, "For their sakes I sanctify myself." As our Scripture put it, "Don't let the world around you squeeze you into its own mold." Say, "I would be pure, for there are those who care." I would keep a love fit to wait for.

When I was courting my wife back in 1952 I wrote a little doggerel poem that expressed how I felt at the time. It was entitled "What Love Is."

> It's getting a thrill from being in the same room with your girl;
> Yet, it's knowing that this feeling isn't just a whirl
> Of sentimental feeling and emotions fiery hot;
> Though these things enter in, in fact contribute quite a lot.
> There are other things: like laughing at the stupids that you pull;
> Like agreeing on the things that make a life that's rich and full.
> It's sharing all your secrets and discussing facts of living;
> It's throwing out the verb "to get" and substituting giving.
> It's laboring, laughing, loving living 'til you reach the final goal…
> A heart of love, a life of peace, and a steady quiet soul.

There is one more dangling preposition. If I were young again, I would have a faith fit to live by. Toward the end of our Scripture Paul says, Base your happiness on your hope in Christ." I haven't put this last, nor did Paul put it last because it's the least important. It's the most important and really I have been talking about it in all that I've said before. When you talk about your self, your work, your love, your life, your faith has already been brought into play. Actually, faith is not just one compartment of life like other compartments. If life is a pie, faith is not just one slice of the pie like other areas of life. Faith is the flavor that shoots through the whole pie and gives every part of the life its zest and meaning. A case in point is this story:

At the 100th anniversary of the arrival of missionaries in Zaire, Christians gathered to celebrate from that part of Zaire once called the Belgian Congo. The festivities lasted all day with music, preaching, food and conversations. Many reminisced about the early days and praised God for the progress of the gospel and the church.

Near the end of the long program, a very old man stood to give a speech. He said that he soon would die and that he needed to tell something that no one else knew. If he didn't tell, his secret would go with him to his grave. He explained that when the first white missionaries came, his people didn't know whether to believe their message or not. So they devised a plan to slowly and secretly poison the missionaries and watch them die. One by one, children and adults became ill, died and were buried. It was when his people saw how these missionaries died that they decided to believe their message.

Think of it — those missionaries never knew what was happening. They didn't know they were being poisoned and they didn't know why they were dying. They didn't know they were martyrs. They stayed and died because they trusted Jesus.

And it was the way they lived and died that taught others how to live.

Oh yes, if I were young again, I would seek a self fit to live with. I'd find a work fit to work at. I'd keep a love fit to wait for. And I'd have a faith fit to live by as I based my happiness on my hope in Christ. Dangle these prepositions through your life and I think you'll find it very much worth living.

Pentecost
A BEWILDERING DAY
Acts 2:1-21

Though at times because of her I have been "Bewitched, bothered and bewildered," this is not a sermon about my wife—A Bewildering Day. But from this exciting story of the beginning of the church on the day of Pentecost, I want us to focus on Luke's telling us that that day was a bewildering day. 2:6 "And at this sound the crowd gathered and was bewildered, because each one heard them speaking in the native language of each."

This had to be bewildering to those folks because they were like so many of us. They had always felt that God's favor rested only on people like themselves. Weren't the Jews God's chosen people? And we've tried to think that the gospel was limited just to people like us. Like the woman out at one of my early churches that saw the ragamuffin children of an alcoholic sharecropper's family that had finally responded to a faithful member's invitation. Saw them right there, sitting in her pew! And she said to me, "They're not our kind of people are they, Brother Watson?"

It made me think about Dr. Fred Craddock's early failure in church work. He was pastor of a beautiful little white country church in the Tennessee Mountains not far out of Oak Ridge where the nuclear experiments were going on. Lots of construction people brought in their trailers all over the backwoods of those mountains and some of them drifted in to the little country church. They were southerners and Yankees, black and white, and first news you know some of them wanted to join the church under Fred's preaching. He was delighted and set up the baptism service. But a week before the service they called a meeting of the board and one member proposed a new by-law. "No one can become a member of this church who is not a permanent resident of this county, and they must have relatives who are members of this church." It passed with one dissenting vote. Fred's.

Years later when he was a teacher of preaching at a Seminary, he passed by that area and wanted to show his wife, Nettie, one of the scenes of his early failures. They drove up into the mountains and sure enough, they found the little church, still beautiful nestled up in its trees, gleaming white. But there was a big sign out in front of it—BARBECUE, ALL YOU CAN EAT. Parking lot full of cars. It was about lunchtime, so Fred said, "Let's go in and eat." They went in and had to wait. There were nice tables and they waited their turn sitting on the pews that had been pushed back up against the wall.

Fred said there were all kinds of people in there, "Parthians, Medes, Elamites, and residents of Mesopotamia, Judea and Cappodocia, Pontus and Asia, Phrygia and Pamphylia,
Egypt and the parts of Libya belonging to Cyrene,
And visitors from Rome and Atlanta and Nashville,
Both Jews and proselytes, Cretans and Arabs."

There was a mixture. Mothers, fathers, grandparents and children, couples and singles were having a good time. After a good barbecue meal they were driving away and Fred said to Nettie, "You know, it may be a good thing that that's no longer a church. Because I don't believe most of those people would be welcome there."

I think that crowd might have also been bewildered because of the kind of people the Holy Spirit was calling into leadership in God's church. Listen to this! 2:17 "In the last days it will be, God declares, that I will pour out my Spirit upon all flesh, and your sons and your daughters shall prophesy…" Daughters prophesying? Isn't that bewildering to a faith that for centuries upon centuries had focused on the patriarchs—Abraham, Isaac, and Jacob?

I may have told you about the incident when one of our Bishops took a real interest in getting a new minister placed in a local church. He even went so far as to give the Pastor Parish Relations Committee the opportunity to interview the pastor he wanted to place there. He was obviously conceding that in effect he was going to give them veto power over the appointment. He even allowed them to invite the minister for a trial sermon. This is very unusual procedure for us Methodists. They'd had a resume of the candidate's credentials and work experience distributed to the committee and had even circulated it throughout the membership. It was such an outstanding resume. The minister came and preached on a Sunday morning when their pastor was out for a vacation break. It went well, very well. The Bishop was going to be out of the country on a Holy Land trip, but he had heard how things were going.

So being pretty confident, he took the unusual step of allowing the committee a final interview with the candidate during which they could tell the preacher whether to count on that appointment being made. The minister showed up for the final interview. They talked a little bit. Everything seemed so congenial. Then the Chair of the Committee began. "We've all seen your resume and it's wonderful. You're really well qualified. We heard you preach; and that was a great sermon. Lots of our young people were really turned on by it. But we've studied it all over; and I regret to inform you that right now in this church's life, we've decided that you're not the one for us."

And she said, "Why?"

Even after all these years some people and churches find it bewildering. Marcia Cochran, Pastor of St. Simon's Island United Methodist Church recalls, "It was 1978. Allison Morgan and I had just been ordained as the first women elders in the South Georgia Conference. I was serving my second year as Associate Pastor at First United Methodist Church in Americus, Georgia. Jimmy Carter was President, so each Sunday we had lots of visitors who were visiting Plains and Sumter County.

During one particular Sunday worship service, I led the congregation in The Apostles' Creed and the prayers. Gene Cariker preached the sermon. We were both dressed in black robes with green stoles.

After the service, I was standing at one of the front doors greeting people when a couple stopped to shake my hand. Noting that they were visitors, I welcomed them to Americus and the church. The woman with a very northern accent said, 'We enjoyed the service today, and I must say how surprised I was to see you. In the north, we don't have women acolytes!'"

The theme of the South Georgia Annual Conference in Savannah a few years back was, "Celebrating Fifty Years of Women in Ministry in South Georgia." Boy, it takes us a while to get over our bewilderment! It has come hard for these women. When Allison Rhodes was sent to her five-point circuit of country churches for her first appointment in the South Georgia Conference, she was one of two women who were ordained for ministry in this conference. It was symbolic that on the first winter Sunday when they fired up the pot-bellied stove, it flushed out a dormant wasp nest from just behind the pulpit in her little country church. All through the sermon she swatted valiantly at the pesky wasps with no offer of help from the congregation. When the service was over, a farmer came up to her in the vestibule and said, "Allison, if you wouldn't swat at them wasps so, they wouldn't sting you." He was really helping her out, wasn't he?

It wasn't the first time that Allison had had trouble with W.A.S.P.s, (White Anglo-Saxon Protestant males). Having grown up in the United Methodist Youth Fellowship at Isle of Hope in Savannah, she had to face the Savannah District Committee on the Ministry to explain her call to the ministry. I was there that day. I served a church in the district and I was on the Committee.

It was a day of shame for me. The District Superintendent shall remain nameless. After being raked over the coals, having her motives impugned, and dire consequences predicted for this improbable venture of clergy-couple ministry with her husband who was also in ministry, she naturally was disturbed and became tearful. Whereupon one of the WASPs concluded, "That's the very reason a woman ought not to be in the ministry. Women just can't control their emotions."

That woman who swatted the wasps now leads a vital ministry of caring as Director of the Cathedral Counseling Center in Atlanta that ironically helps ministers and people to get control of their emotions in the most positive way. She persevered as a pioneer for women in ministry and has lived to see probably about forty or fifty of her sisters in service in this conference. And they're not just in places like Bloomfield where Ceil Mitchell is serving. Leigh Ann Raynor is Senior Pastor at First Church Thomasville. I've quoted her several times in sermons I've delivered. Of course, United Methodist Women, always out ahead of the men, had been pushing for the "Status and Role of Women" in our society for more than a hundred years before this happened.

You wouldn't think you'd have to push so hard for something that the Holy Spirit inaugurated at the very beginning of the church, would you? I remember how all the Methodist churches in Savannah had a Sunday Night Sing and as a part of the program the Savannah Korean Methodist Choir sang in their own language great anthems and hymns. The people attending who didn't know a word of Korean heard and understood the praise of God in their own language. We shouldn't be surprised. The explanation is the Holy Spirit at Pentecost. From the birthday of the church, people from all nations under heaven were there and were able to comprehend the gospel.

What about that workshop at Palen United Methodist Church, a primarily black congregation—the descendants of slaves hosting the whole Savannah District UMW on the theme, "Celebrating our Differences?" How do you explain that in the Deep South? Could it be, "Even upon my slaves, both men and women, in those days I will pour out my Spirit, and they shall prophesy?" (Acts 2:18)

Daughters are prophesying. Joyce Payne, one of our Conference Evangelists, served the little Laurel Branch Church with distinction before I went there, and brought them back from the brink of extinction at a critical time in its history. Two outstanding black women, Brenda Iglehart and Beverly Flowers are now pastors of the largest historically black Methodist congregations in Savannah. Denise Walton is District Superintendent of the Dublin District. And did you know that thirty to forty percent of the students in our school of theology now are women.

God said it, "I will pour out my spirit upon all flesh, and your sons and your daughters shall prophesy." (Acts 2:17) All of this holds out hope to us because Pentecost is not just a memory of the church as to how it began, but it's a vision of what it ought to be and an explanation of all the marvelous things that are happening in its life now. For that, I don't think any of us should mind being a little bit bewildered.

July 4th/Independence Day
WHAT DO THESE STONES MEAN?
Genesis 1:27, Joshua 4:19-24

What's the purpose of observing our national holiday— Independence Day, July 4th? Your first thought might be, "Why that's simple and even ridiculous for the preacher to ask, for it's simply a time to renew our patriotism and our love of country and the flag. Everybody knows that. It's a time to remember stories like the one about the South Georgia Boy who was returning into New York Harbor after three years of fighting in the European Theatre of War. As the ship approached the Statue of Liberty, which was looking out to sea, he said, "Old gal, you ain't never gonna' see me again unless you turn around."

Surely on such a day it's appropriate to recall such love of homeland and country which has been exhibited by millions of young people in service across the history of this nation. And yet all of us know we aren't to use this day just to cultivate blind patriotism, for an uninformed, blind patriotism is subject to perversions. We don't want to be like Stephen Decatur, a politician of another generation that said, "My country, in her intercourse with all the nations of the earth, may she always be in the right—but my country right or wrong!" Instead it's better for us to remember Abraham Lincoln. One day when the civil war was raging its worst, a minister said to Lincoln, "I surely hope the Lord is on our side."

Lincoln said, "I am not at all concerned about that, for I know that the Lord is always on the side of the right; but it is my constant anxiety and prayer that I and this nation should be on the Lord's side."

How then shall we use this day? This incident in the founding of the Hebrew nation could give us a clue. Joshua had the people take up twelve stones out of the bed of the

Jordan River when they crossed over it. And when they got settled in Gilgal, Joshua set them up as a monument and said, "When your children ask their parents in time to come, 'What do these stones mean?' then you shall let your children know, 'Israel crossed over the Jordan here on dry ground.' Why did he ask them to do this? "So that all the peoples of the earth may know that the hand of the Lord is mighty, and so that you may stand in awe of the Lord your God forever."

The Flag, The 4th of July, the fireworks—these are our twelve stones. Hopefully our children will ask, "What do these stones mean?" And we can say, "It's a day of memory of those who have gone before us—those who at great sacrifice carved out the heritage we enjoy." All of you remember the old story of the bored little boy asking his mother back during World War II about the flag in the sanctuary with stars on it signifying young men and women who had died in the service of their country. He said, "Momma, what's that flag for?"

She said, "Son, that's the flag for the boys that died in the service."

He said, "Which one, Momma, the morning or the evening service?"

This is a day for the boys and the girls that have really died in the service. The twelve hours of daylight ought to be for us twelve stones that remind us of their sacrifice.

One Fourth of July Sunday the treasurer of the church reported to the preacher that a family in the church that had lost their son in the war had given $200 to the church in his memory. The preacher told his wife about it. She said, "Let's give $200 for our son."

The preacher said, "Our son didn't die in the war."

She said, "No, he didn't. All the more reason that we ought to give in gratitude." These twelve stones remind us of those who have crossed over Jordan and given the last full measure of devotion.

When your children ask their parents in time to come, "What do these stones mean?" Then you shall say, "This celebration is a call for communication between the generations about our heritage and destiny as a nation under God."

We take a clue again here from Lincoln. Some wag said that Lincoln wrote the Gettysburg address "while riding from Washington to Gettysburg on the back of an envelope." Actually, he rode on a train, I think. But he concluded it with these words,

"that from these honored dead we take increased devotion to that cause for which they gave the last full measure of devotion—that we here highly resolve that these dead shall not have died in vain—that this nation, under God, shall have a new birth of freedom, and that government of the people, by the people, for the people shall not perish from the earth."

We're not just remembering those who went before us, but we have a new dedication to the freedom for which they died.

What do these stones mean? They mean that we keep working. I know Jefferson said in the Declaration of Independence, "We hold these truths to be self-evident. That all men are created equal, that they are endowed by their creator with certain unalienable rights—that among these are life, liberty, and the pursuit of happiness." But they are obviously not self-evident to everybody. They are not self-perpetuating. They have to be protected in every generation from those who in the name of security would take away even from an American citizen the right to face his or her accusers and be represented fairly in a court of law.

What do these stones mean? They mean we have to keep working as a nation to fully realize that dream voiced by Emma Lazarus, a Jewish refugee from Europe, whose words are carved at the base of the Statue of Liberty,

"Give me your tired, your poor,
Your huddled masses yearning to breathe free,
The wretched refuse of your teeming shore,
Send these, the homeless, tempest tossed to me.
I lift my lamp beside the golden door."

What do these stones mean? They mean we have to keep moving toward the realization of the dream contained in Lincoln's Second Inaugural when he said,

"With malice toward none, with charity for all, with firmness in the right as God gives us to see the right, let us strive on to finish the work we are in, to bind up the nation's wounds—to do all which may achieve and cherish a just and lasting peace among ourselves and with all nations."

I emailed my lawyer son, Wade, because he's something of a history buff, and I asked him to give me the top ten reasons he was grateful to be an American. He was busy, so he wrote back and said,

Three reasons I'm glad I live in the U.S.A.: 1) Benjamin Franklin, 2) John Adams, 3) Alexander Hamilton.

I said, "Son, I've got to have more than that."

So he wrote back and said, "Daddy. Benjamin Franklin: Personified the idea of the dignity of the working middle class and its capacity to rise to greatness when given freedom and opportunity. Franklin's life has been the model of every American rags to riches story. He arrived in Philadelphia penniless and with little formal education, only to rise to become America's wealthiest publisher and leading diplomat.

John Adams: Understood and promoted the idea of the absolute necessity of having an independent judiciary to maintain liberty. A brilliant lawyer, he successfully defended the British soldiers accused of murder in the infamous Boston massacre by convincing the jury that the soldiers acted in self-defense against an unruly mob. "Facts are stubborn things," he said.

Alexander Hamilton: Conceived and advocated a strong national government tempered by a balance of powers. Hamilton knew Lord Compton's phrase, "Power corrupts, and absolute power corrupts absolutely." So if we remain a free nation we'll never be free of the constant jockeying for powers between the Executive Branch—the President, the Legislative Branch—the Congress, and the Judicial Branch—the Courts.

When you see the hassle in the news between these branches, don't despair. Rejoice, for it's in these very arguments and the balance of powers that our freedom lies. Start worrying when you see no argument with the Executive Branch. (See The Federalist Papers) Hamilton also created the framework of a national financial system, which has proven over the last 200 years to be the most successful in the world.

Wade said, "These ideas made the U.S.A. unique in the 18th century and they continue to define our national character today." But I still didn't have quite enough, so I had to do some thinking on my own.

I couldn't leave out Thomas Jefferson even if he did father a child by one of his slaves. It's an established matter of record that he fathered children by his slave, Sally Hemings. I couldn't leave him out because he wrote the Declaration of Independence. That document was bigger than him and the hardened customs of his generation. "We hold these truths to be self evident, that all men are created equal, that they are endowed by their creator with certain unalienable rights, that among these are life, liberty, and the pursuit of happiness. That to secure these rights governments are instituted among men, deriving their just powers from the consent of the governed." All equal, endowed by creator. (Genesis 1:27) Those two ideas were so big they finally brought down the slavery he hung on to in his lifetime.

George Washington was big enough to see it. Before Abraham Lincoln came along to enforce it with The Emancipation Proclamation, he knew slavery had to go before the onslaught of those ideas. At his death, in his will, George Washington, the Father of our Country, freed all his slaves.

And "governments deriving their just powers from the consent of the governed." He might not have realized how far it would go... even women getting the right to vote, even those freed slaves getting the right to vote. The Declaration, and the Constitution written by James Madison having within them such big ideas of freedom that we haven't yet extended them to all to whom they belong. But in this "Land of the Free and the Home of the Brave" we believe that they'll all finally fully realize these freedoms because they are "endowed by their creator with these unalienable rights."

Our founders even created the Bill of Rights with those goodies in them like "Congress shall make no law with respect to the establishment of a religion nor prohibiting the free exercise thereof"... Freedom of the Press, Freedom of Speech, Freedom to assemble peacefully...To be free in our homes and persons from unreasonable search or seizures without probable cause or a warrant. I'm grateful for this Bill of Rights that now totals 27 Amendments to the Constitution just spelling out in situation after situation our rights.

But, you know, every right carries with it a responsibility. With all this freedom, what gave the founders the confidence to believe that we wouldn't just have anarchy with "every man just doing what was right in his own eyes," as the Bible puts it. I think they had the wisdom to foresee that they didn't have to worry about that—that they'd have people like you readers coming along to create responsible citizens that would be able to handle the freedom that was purchased for us at so great a price

What does this day really mean to you—this Fourth of July? Does it mean to us what it did to our founders? My friend Thomas Lane Butts made me aware that John Adams, statesman and second president of the United States, was determined to live until the 50th anniversary of the signing of the Declaration of Independence – July 4, 1826. At dawn on that day he was awakened by his servant, who asked if he knew what day it was. He replied: "Oh yes, it is the glorious Fourth of July. God bless it. God bless you all." He then slipped into a coma. In the afternoon he recovered consciousness briefly to murmur, "Thomas Jefferson lives." These were his last words.

Unbeknownst to him, Thomas Jefferson had died earlier that same day. It is reported that on the evening of July 3rd, Thomas Jefferson was in bed and his life ebbing rapidly. He whispered to a young friend who was watching by his bedside: "Is this the fourth?" The man could not bring himself to say that it was not yet, so kept silent. Jefferson repeated the question and this time the friend nodded. A look of deep satisfaction came over Jefferson's face, he sighed deeply, lay back, sank into a deep sleep, and died shortly after noon on the fourth.

It is remarkable that these two brilliant statesmen, whose resolve had so much to do with laying the foundation of our republic, were able to stay alive until they could celebrate that date so precious to them both. If you are a student of the philosophy of "life after life," or if you use your imagination to put some content into your Christian understanding of life after death, or if you have some bewonderment about what happens and who we see when we die, then you will enjoy thinking about John Adams' comment, "Thomas Jefferson lives" as he left this world. Jefferson had preceded Adams in death by a few hours. Did these two meet up as they left on the "long journey"?

Could I suggest to all of us that we don't have to die today to truly celebrate the Fourth? I think we can ask of Flag, and Fireworks, and Freedom and our Faith, "What do these stones mean?" And then go forth to work to realize the dream so that we "may stand in awe of the Lord our God forever."

Christian Education Sunday[1]
SOMETHING NEVER OUT OF DATE
Ruth 1:1-18, Matthew 5:17-20

When I was eight or nine years old my cousin, Dennis, from the big city of Philadelphia came to visit me in Baxley, Georgia and I was showing him around town, roaming as little boys will do. We came to one of my favorite places, a blacksmith shop where the smithy would take the red-hot horseshoe from the bellows and bang it into shape on the heavy anvil before it cooled and hardened. The smell of the hot metal mingled with the odor of the horses waiting to be shod. In those days we had two big livery stables in Baxley where mules were kept and sold for farming and horses were used for pleasure by a number of families in town. When my older cousin saw that bellows and anvil and mallet—the whole operation of the blacksmith shop, he said, "Boy, is that thing ever out of date!"

I didn't know then how right he was, for by the time I reached High School the livery stables were gone and the blacksmith shop was gone, replaced by the tractor and the automobile; and the smell of the animals no longer wafted its way over the town.

We're still facing the onslaught of technology that changes our way of life. We can resist it like most of us want to resist the advance of the computer age. Few of us have escaped the bill-mailing computer that makes a mistake, and you write it and write it, never getting any answer except threatening letters. We've been folded, spindled and mutilated by bill-writing computers. Art Buchwald, the columnist, tells of a mythical fellow named McDonald who, refusing to forgive an arrogant

[1] The Annual Celebration in the Church School when students move up to new classes, perhaps receive a Bible with their name on it; and Church School Teachers are rededicated to their tasks.

and then contrite computer, finally informed it that he was deceased and had willed his money to science to develop a way of transplanting a human heart into a cold computer.

But we know the computer is here to stay or to be replaced by something even more amazing. Dr. Glen Burton of our Experiment Station at Tifton said that he worked on a math problem for two days before he had the answer for a research project. After that, he went to the University of Georgia and just for fun fed the same problem into the super computer there. He got the answer in two seconds.

Our daughter, Susan, loves to tell about the yard sale in Albany, Georgia where a little boy about seven or so found a typewriter and was so proud when he talked his parents into buying it for him. He said, "I have heard of these." We look now at an old adding machine, a marvel in its time, and say, "Boy is that thing ever out of date!"

Some in Jesus day were obviously saying the same thing about the old Jewish Law, the "law and the prophets." They thought that since the advent of Jesus, the Messiah, there was no longer any need to obey the endless commandments and moral codes that had evolved over the centuries among the people of God. You can understand why they might have believed that. After all, hadn't Paul said, "It is no longer I that live, but Christ that lives in me, and the life I now live in the flesh, I live by faith in the Son of God who loved me and gave himself for me?" In the Christian era weren't legal codes to be replaced by an indwelling spirit? Didn't Jesus himself say in other contexts that all the law and the prophets hang on two commandments: "Love the Lord your God with all your heart" and "You shall love your neighbor as yourself?" Isn't this so much simpler?

And Jesus, what about your saying that simplest of all behavior summaries, "In everything do to others as you would have them do to you; for this is the law and the prophets?" It's no wonder we get confused and think there's no longer any need to fool with that old stuff, that law, those commandments, those ancient stories, those prophetic utterances. Those efforts to spell out in daily life detail the implications for a life that has chosen life by obeying the commandments of the Lord God are just passé now. We look at the law and say, "Is that thing ever out of date!"

Whenever and wherever this happens, Jesus knows he has to assert a corrective. So he says, "Do not think that I have come to abolish the law or the prophets; I have come not to abolish but to fulfill. For truly I tell you, until heaven and earth pass away, not one letter, not one stroke of a letter, will pass from the law until all is accomplished. Therefore, whoever breaks one of the least of these commandments, and teaches others to do the same, will be called least in the kingdom of heaven; but whoever does them and teaches them will be called great in the kingdom of heaven."

Jesus says there'll never come a time in human history when it's not necessary to teach the commandments and ideas that are the practical application of the law of love for God and neighbor. We talk about new morality and situation ethics, but both of these claim to make love central. They don't go a single step beyond Jesus who made love and what happens to your neighbor central in all his teaching and living. No matter what progress we have and no matter how many new things appear on the human horizon, there'll always be a need for dedicated teachers of the faith who do and teach these commandments. "Whoever does them and teaches them will be called great in the kingdom of heaven."

Think about Ruth in the Old Testament. She was a foreigner, a Moabite, Gentile woman who became the great-great-great-great grandmother of Jesus Christ. Look at this widowed Ruth who was so loyal to her mother-in-law that she threw off her pleas to go back to her homeland where she could be safe and cared for. She said, "Entreat me not to leave thee, nor to seek from following after thee, for whither thou goest I will go and where thou lodgest I will lodge. Thy people shall be my people and thy God my God."

This Ruth used a sickle to gather the wheat left in the field for the poor. Now we've improved upon Ruth's sickle. If she came back today, we'd put her sickle in a museum. We have machines that storm across the fields and harvest more in an hour than Ruth with her sickle could harvest in a lifetime. We've improved upon Ruth's sickle, but have we improved upon Ruth—upon her loyalty and love? I don't think so. There won't be a time in human history when children and youth and adults don't need to be reminded of what Ruth did and what that means for our life today.

We've learned to fly the air like birds, to burrow the ground like moles, to swim the sea like fish, and even how to travel between planets like comets; but we haven't yet learned how to walk the earth like humans. As Bertrand Russell put it, "Our problem is not whether we can occupy space, it's whether we can continue to occupy this planet." As the song put it,

> "What the world needs now is love sweet love;
> That's the only thing that there's just too little of."

And every generation needs to be shown it and told it afresh.

"Ma," my mother-in-law, told me before she died about being in a new antique shop out of Greensboro, North

Carolina with her niece, Mary Morecock. As you can imagine, these two ladies were having a ball. They were going about from item to item enthusiastically commenting on everything there. It was full of the most beautiful china and old silver and cut glass. "Ma" would say to Mary, "And here is a tea pitcher."

Mary would say to Ma, "Here's a fantastic old sugar bowl." And so they went on in avid conversation naming off item after item.

"And here's a gravy boat."

"And here's a cake keeper."

Suddenly through all their chatter they heard a little voice say, "And here's a little girl!"

They looked down and saw a little girl with pencil and pad, drawing pictures. She was a child of the neighborhood who was accustomed to being in the shop every day who was afraid she was not going to be noticed by these ladies who were so overwhelmed by the glamorous offerings of the shop.

With all the flashing glamour and abundance of technological progress in our time, it's easy for us to get carried away and fail to notice that right at our feet, looking up to be seen and noticed and heard, is a new generation—"And here's a little girl! And here are fifteen babies, and here's a husky youth, and here's a young adult, and here are a group of aging seniors all needing to learn the applied message of love for our time."

Oh it's true. There are some things that you look at and say; "Boy is that thing ever out of date!" But there must be some things that are never out of date because he said, "Until heaven and earth pass away, not one letter, not one stroke of a letter, will pass from the law (of love) until all is accomplished." And if you have a part in doing love, and teaching love, you will be called great in the kingdom of heaven.

❖

Labor Day/Sunday
WORK IS SACRED, TOO
Deuteronomy 24:14-15, Colossians 3:23

Labor Day is a holiday honoring working people. More than a hundred years ago, Peter J. McGuire, founder of the United Brotherhood of Carpenters, suggested a special day to pay tribute to the country's working people. President Cleveland signed a bill making Labor Day a legal holiday in 1894. It is well, for our faith has always sought to protect the rights of working people while it has urged commitment to excellence in work based on our faith commitment. The book of Deuteronomy announced an amazing labor policy when we consider that it was written about 1000 B.C. It says:

"You shall not oppress a hired servant who is poor and needy, whether he is one of your brethren or one of the sojourners who are in your land within your towns, you shall give him his hire on the day he earns it, before the sun goes down (for he is poor and sets his heart upon it); lest he cry against you to the Lord, and it be sin in you."

Then Paul speaks of several vocations from the highest down to the lowly servant and he says:
"Whatever you are doing, put your whole heart into it as if you were doing it for the Lord and not for men."
Fair treatment of laboring people. Wholehearted work at the jobs we do.

"Build a steeple on the barn," the woman said, "and put a cross at the top." I think it was Martha Berry out from Rome, Georgia. She was founding a home and school for the underprivileged, and this was one of her specifications. "I know it's not a church," she explained, as the carpenter stared in surprise. "But when the boys are in the field plowing and they look toward the barn, I want them to remember that their work is sacred also!"

That's something to remember as we celebrate Labor Day.

The Feast of Tabernacles/Booths[2]
LEST WE FORGET
Deut. 8:7-18, Lev. 23:33-34, 39, Neh. 8:17, Isa 45:1,4, Hosea 2:14-15

When the British Empire was at its zenith at the celebration of the sixtieth anniversary of the reign of Queen Victoria, high government officials and troops from all the colonies of the Empire, and nearly two hundred vessels of the Royal Navy were assembled for the ceremonies. It was then that Rudyard Kipling sounded a warning to a nation dazzled by the pomp and splendor of the occasion. We used to sing these words in an anthem I directed as Minister of Music at my first church job in Griffin, Georgia. Kipling said:

> The tumult and the shouting dies;
> The Captains and the Kings depart:
> Still stands Thine ancient sacrifice,
> A humble and a contrite heart.
> Lord God of Hosts, be with us yet,
> Lest we forget—lest we forget!

Kipling wasn't the first to sound such a warning. When the Israelites "had eaten their fill and had built fine houses, when their herds and flocks had multiplied, when their silver and

---

[2] This Special Day celebrated by our Jewish Friends near the end of September or the beginning of October is appropriate to be included because of the long-standing Friendship in Macon of Christians with Jews in support of the programs of Macon Outreach. In Savannah, Georgia, such a friendship exists between Temple Mickve Israel and Wesley Monumental UMC that dates back to the founding of Savannah. These congregations across the years have offered each other their facilities when they were burned out or experienced other calamities. Rabbis have often shared at Wesley Family Nights showing the details and significance of Passover Observance and other High Holy days in their faith.

gold had multiplied, and all that they had was multiplied," Moses said to them: "Take care that you do not forget the Lord your God. Do not say to yourself, 'My Power and the might of my own hand have gotten me this wealth.' But remember!'" (Deut. 8:11, 17-18)

A lot of us need to remember. My son-in-law must have thought it was important to remember. I think he's achieved quite a bit for a young man. After serving for several years as Pastor of the largest churches in our Conference, he's Director of New Congregational Development and Revitalizing Churches for our Annual Conference. In addition to that, he out-married himself. He wooed and won our first-born, and together they have produced two out of the five most remarkable grandchildren in the nation. I say this as a totally unbiased observer. But somehow, Tim thought it was important to remember his origins and how it all got started.

So he planned a little celebration on August 28, their anniversary, as a complete surprise to our daughter, Susan. He went to the trouble to transcribe their wedding ceremony off of an old reel to reel tape that I had made when they married at Bainbridge in 1976 so he could play the original music of their wedding right up to the vows. Then he imported the two officiating ministers, his father, The Rev. John Bagwell, and me, and we re-enacted the ceremony, this time with his son, John Hampton, and daughter, Emily Day, serving as best man and maid of honor to their father and mother. Then he had it so well planned. Day and I would serve as child sitters while they retraced the steps of their original honeymoon.

They went to the New Perry Hotel for supper, then to the Macon Hilton, then to Unicoi State Park out from Helen, Georgia in the wilderness, in a little Quonset hut, where they spent their first days together as a couple. Though the analogy breaks down a little bit, because Tim and Susan have always loved and been loyal to each other, it made me think about what the prophet Hosea had God saying to his nation Israel that had lost its first love and gone after other gods:

"Therefore I will now allure her and bring her into the wilderness, and speak tenderly to her. There she shall respond as in the days of her youth, as at the time when she came out of the land of Egypt." (Hosea 2:14-15)

I think Tim must have had something like that in mind. Through remembrance and re-enactment, he wanted to recapture the love they first had for each other when it was not based on possessions or achievement or success or anything that he had done, or even anything that they had done together. He wanted to affirm a pristine, given as a gift from God, relationship of love and trust and commitment and responsibility.

And so the Jews celebrated the Feast of Booths, or the feast of Tabernacles. The booths or tabernacles were for them symbols of their time in the wilderness when they were brought through—preserved by God to form a great nation. Leviticus has God saying, (23:42-43)

"You shall live in booths for seven days, so that your generations may know that I made the people of Israel live in booths when I brought them out of the land of Egypt. I am the Lord your God!"

In the time of Nehemiah, he made it a celebration of the return of Israel from the exile in Babylon. So, Nehemiah 8:17:

"And all the assembly of those who had returned from the captivity made booths, and lived in them; for from the days of Jeshua, son of Nun, to that day the people of Israel had not done so. And there was very great rejoicing."

Our holidays like Thanksgiving and the 4th of July, Independence Day, are similar celebrations, lest we forget— lest we forget the sacrifices of those patriots who launched this nation against seemingly insurmountable odds.

Lest we forget! Lest we forget! There is the ongoing need in our time to remember. I know there's a saying, "Forgive and Forget." But the Jews of our century have discovered that that's wrong. More accurately it should be, "Remember and forgive!" For only as we remember does the forgiveness have any content to it or any integrity about it.

The Jews make a big deal today out of remembering the Holocaust. You'd think they would want to forget it. What a horrible thing to hold always before your life and your children, the systematic elimination of over six million Jews by Gentiles whose descendants we have now embraced as those who have torn down the Berlin Wall to be reunited. And we might well embrace some of them, for all of them didn't participate in Hitler's horror.

The Rev. Penelope Duckworth, Chaplain at Stanford University, tells how years ago, on a night flight from New York to the West Coast, she went up to the lounge of the huge 747 to get a Coke. An older woman with an Eastern European accent asked if she could join her. As they talked, the woman asked Penelope about her family, and then began to tell Penelope about hers. Her son was a teacher in Boston and her daughter lived on a kibbutz in Israel. From this, Penelope assumed that the woman was Jewish, and when she made a remark to that effect, the woman explained that she was a Christian but that she had raised her daughter as a Jew. When Penelope asked her why she had done that, she told this story.

When the Nazis came to her village in Poland to round up the Jews for transport to the camps, nobody really knew what was happening but everybody sensed something dreadful. The smell of death was in the air. She was doing her weekly shopping near the train station the day the Nazis arrived. Gestapo Officers were pushing the Jewish villagers onto the trains and one was pushing a woman who had a little girl with her. He turned to the Jewish woman, pointed to her daughter and said, "Is this your daughter?"

The woman stopped, and looking straight at this Christian woman that she didn't even know, she said, "No, the child is hers."

Penelope said, "And so you took her daughter?"

She said, "Yes, what would you have done"

What would we have done?

I believe this. Only as Jews remember the Holocaust does their loyal participation in and contribution to our common life have any content and integrity to it. Only in this way does it become remarkable. Before I left Savannah, I remember reading an article about a Mr. Cohen who founded the Builderama Chain, which fell on evil days after he sold it. But while he had it, it was one of the finest, fastest growing businesses of the area, similar to Lowe's and Home Depot now. I recall how the article spoke of his support for the Jewish Educational Alliance, but it also told how he became the champion for public education in that area for all people, black, white, bronze and brown. He wanted all ethnic groups in our midst to be prepared for a more abundant life. Forgive and forget? No! Remember and forgive! Remember the Holocaust, and forgiveness and participation in life like that have content to them!

I suggest that as the Jews celebrate their Feast of Booths that we join them. Some might think such a celebration is archaic and unnecessary in our generation. Nothing like the

Red Sea deliverance ever happens anymore. The age of miracle deliverance by God is over. It stopped at the edge of the waters of the sea of reeds at the time of Moses. It's silly for our Jews to go out in the back yard and build booths or tents and live in them like they did when they were living in the wilderness on their way to the Promised Land. But I don't know about that. Is the age of miracle deliverance by God over? Could anyone have predicted in our generation the rise of a leader like Gorbachev, maybe the Cyrus of our time?

You remember how Cyrus, the great Persian King, rose to deliver the Jews from exile in Babylon? And Isaiah has God saying to this pagan ruler,

"Thus says the Lord to his anointed, to Cyrus, whose right hand I have grasped to subdue nations before him and strip kings of their robes—to open doors before him, and the gates shall not be closed. I call you by your name. I surname you though you do not know me." (Isaiah 45:1,4)

Could Gorbachev have been like Cyrus, used by God though he didn't know him or acknowledge him?

Since the rise of communism in Russia over 114 years ago, the whole world had been held in a bondage more threatening than the taskmasters of Egypt ever imposed on their Hebrew slaves. We weren't guided by a "pillar of cloud by day and a pillar of fire by night." Instead the threat of a mushroom cloud hung over us for over 40 years in our wilderness. There in that wilderness a totalitarian, monolithic giant, the Soviet Union, and a hodgepodge of NATO Nations were squared off with much more threatening weapons than Goliath or David ever carried in their arsenals.

Which of us planned or could have predicted the fall of the Berlin Wall when it tumbled down—"When the walls came a tumblin' down?" Who among us thought that a leader who rose up from within their own brainwashed ranks would undertake the dismantling of the whole communistic, socio-economic, military system?

I tell you what we ought to do—what we really ought to do. I remember living in Colquitt, Georgia during the Kruschev-Kennedy Cuban missile crisis. A lot of us were building a "Fall-out Shelter" in the basements of our churches. I don't know why we felt we had to do that. We already had "Shell-out Falter" every time the offering plate was passed in our churches. Why did we need a "Fall-out Shelter"? At my house we even stored up canned water and peanut butter that we put in a closet at the very center of our house to tide us over when the great mushroom cloud finally burst over us. And we envisioned ourselves as perhaps the only surviving families of a nuclear bombed-out generation.

We ought to get up our own Feast of Booths in our homes. We ought to go to the center of our houses and live for a week in a fall-out shelter again and thank God that the days of miraculous deliverance by God are not over.

Oh there is still some uncertainty—the terrorism hanging over from 9/11 and the threat of new wars are real. And even as we thank God for the beginnings of our nation in the past, we wonder if we in our church are going to have a role to play in this 21st century. Who knows but what today with the few of us who read this, God may be about to work a new miracle deliverance of deeper dedication that leads to another century of service to whatever communities our heirs now find themselves living within? We don't know what the future holds, but we know who holds the future. And we can stop right now on our Feast of Booths, and thank God who is still:

The deliverer from the bondage that binds us,
The provider of the bounty that blesses us,

The Father of the Son who saves us,
The creator of all, who still has "The Whole World in His Hands."

> The tumult and the shouting dies;
> The captains and the kings depart:
> Still stands Thine ancient sacrifice,
> An humble and a contrite heart.
> Lord God of Hosts, be with us yet,
> Lest we forget—lest we forget! Forget!

Stewardship/Pledge Sunday
AN EXAMPLE THAT YOU SHOULD FOLLOW
I Peter 2:19-25, I Corinthians 16:2

What do you say when you're writing to people who are already evidencing their commitment as significant givers and tithers?

I guess there's just one major question I want to ask and try to answer. If we have become committed proportionate givers, if we have become that kind of person that offers service in concrete ways to Christ and the church and the community, if we have become committed Christian people, what would have caused it to happen? How would it come to be? What would be the forces that have motivated us? How does it happen if we come to be committed people?

Does it happen because we get a sudden windfall or become more prosperous and then decide, "Well now I can afford to tithe or give to the church."? Or, "I'm not busy. I've got a lot of free time on my hands now, so I can do some volunteer things. Back when we were scraping the bottom of the budget, winding up with too much month at the end of our money, with our noses to the grindstone, it was impossible to tithe or give service. But now it's possible!" Is that the way it happens?

A man was asked, "What would you do if you had a million dollars?"
And he said, "I'd pay my debts, as far as it went!"
Oh I think we'd find something else to do with the money or time if that's all that happened, wouldn't we?

My in-laws, Ben and Jane, Day's sister and husband, were challenged at a family supper at the church to tithe for just three months, and to do it on a weekly basis. Much emphasis was placed on weekly giving, for giving is an act of worship and should be performed on the same regular basis as church attendance. As Paul put it, (I Cor. 16:2), "On the first day of the week each of you is to set something aside as he may prosper."

So they went home, discussed this challenge and finally decided they would give it a try. Ben had a pretty good job for that day, but their total income was $600 per month with two boys, and the first of each month usually brought on a major crisis as they tried to stretch to pay all of their bills. It was in this context that they made a decision to take their first $60 each month, divide it into weekly increments of $15 to give to the church and see if they could struggle through 90 days like that. Ben says, "After three months the question of continuing never came up, and 50 years later neither of us has ever suggested stopping." Now why did they do that? It wasn't any windfall of prosperity.

Do we become committed givers and servers because we believe it will pay off for us? Do we tithe because we think it will pay off in prosperity or contentment? Oh I know some Scripture seems to suggest this. The prophet Malachi has God saying, "Bring the full tithes into the storehouse... and put me to the test if I will not open the windows of heaven for you and pour down for you an overflowing blessing."(3:10)

True enough! I've quoted John Templeton, the Dean of global investing in this country, who was asked what was the best risk-free investment, and he said, "To tithe."

He said, "In my 46 years of experience I have never known anyone who regretted that investment." He said, "I have never known anyone who has made that investment for ten years without being rewarded with both happiness and prosperity."

But can this be the motivation? Doesn't that have to come as a surprise or a bonus or serendipity? And isn't it true that while ultimate satisfaction and contentment may be there, and no regrets, doesn't some people's total commitment lead them to a cross of suffering like their Lord's?

And what if you calculate to go directly after it like Simon the Sorcerer. You remember him? He tried to buy the gift of the Spirit and healing power from Peter and John. (Acts 8:8-21) But Peter said to him, "Your silver perish with you because you thought you could obtain the gift of God with money. You have neither part nor lot in this matter, for your heart is not right before God."

I don't believe anybody ever becomes a real committed giver and server just because they believe it'll pay off for them—that they can strike a deal with God, that they can bargain with the Almighty for a mess of pottage! I believe that there has to be some higher motivation for it to last or it'll go out the window with the first market crash or recession, or the first illness, or the first loss of a job.

Do people become committed tithers or givers and servers because they believe the church needs their money and time; that it's doing a great, compassionate work in the name of Christ and is therefore worthy of their support? In John 14:12, Jesus says, "He who believes in me will also do the works that I do; and greater works than these will he do because I go to my Father." Jesus was limited to Palestine and a few acts of healing, but his church will do greater things: vast numbers of hospitals and child-care centers, children's homes, Vashties for troubled adolescents, Wesley Glen for mentally challenged adults, Magnolia Manors for the elderly, Mulberry Street Outreach... all in the name of Christ.

Through cooperation with World Church Councils his church can bring aid to over 100 million hungry and earthquake and flood distraught and war scarred refugees across this world. To care for the retired ministers, the soldiers of the cross and their spouses and widows, to provide Christian nurture, education, and pastoral care at the local level! Oh the church needs our money to carry on the causes of Christ, to deploy our 670 missionaries to win the world for Him. I'm sure that motivates some of us.

But not everybody believes that every dollar goes for what they want it to. You remember one year's Mother's Day Ad Campaign for Magnolia Manor featuring my son-in-law, Tim Bagwell, and his mother B. Nell? Can't you imagine that some people thought to themselves, "Why should I give money to support a healthy woman and her husband who can travel in a camper all over the country? And on top of that, doesn't that boy have one of the top jobs in the Conference? Why doesn't he look after his own parents?"

Others might think, "Why should we be paying to keep up a place so that wealthy elders from wherever can take their estates out of the tax base of revenue starved cities and live in a plush environment?"

When Vance Mathis was pastor at Mulberry, they were in their stewardship campaign, and a fellow said to him after the service, "I don't agree with you. Furthermore, I don't trust the United Methodist Church or the Women's Division of Christian Service, or the Board of Global Ministries. And I'm suspicious of Emory University where you graduated. I think the Bishop and the District Superintendents and the Cabinet are just a bunch of hungry powerbrokers!"

And then Vance said, "He began to get negative."

The truth is, if we're depending on 100% agreement on every cause that the church pursues and the absolute belief that the church needs that money and time, not too many people will become committed tithers, givers and servers.

How does it happen? If it happens in your life, what caused it to happen, or what would have caused it to happen?

I'd like to believe that a well planned campaign, or my great preaching would cause my hearers to make a decision that would change their lives and cause them to give of themselves in service and gifts, not until it hurt, but until it quit hurting and began to bless. But I have to admit that if such a thing happens, the roots of it are way before any campaign. Though our text was written to help Christians in Peter's day to endure suffering, the reason it's the central text of what I'm getting at is because it points to the two most important motivational roots that cause anybody to become a committed giver and server.

Do you see it in this Scripture? "For to this you have been called, because Christ also suffered for you, leaving you an example that you should follow in his steps."

How does it happen if we come to be committed people?

We are called to commitment because of an EXAMPLE. Albert Schweitzer said, "Influence is not the main thing that causes us to lead the Christian life; it is the only thing." Leaving you an example that you should follow in his steps.

The Greek word for example means "a child's writing copy." It's "hupogrammos," a word that comes from the way in which children were taught to write in the ancient world. At the top of the writing exercise book there was a copy-head of copperplate handwriting, and the child had to copy the letters out on the line below. Example!

In my last large church, when 16 of our families pledged an average of over $8,000 each at the Steering Committee pledge service, one of our leaders told us why he was a committed giver today. As a little child—6 or 7 or 8, the family was faced with a crisis. They didn't have enough money to get clothes and some of the other things they thought were necessities, and child that he was, he spotted a big roll of bills in his mama's pocketbook. He said, "What do you mean we don't have any money? Look at all that money."

But his mother said, "Hush! That's the tithe. That's the Lord's. That's already committed to the church, and it's going Sunday."

And our leader said, "That left a profound impression on me, and I don't ever remember after that making a conscious decision to tithe. When I got my own income, it just seemed to be the right thing to do." Example!

And the other root? How do we come to be committed people? "For to this you have been called, because Christ also suffered for you." The other root is the GRATITUDE we feel for the grace of Christ. We have received a great gift. How else can we respond to it except to give?

> Were the whole realm of nature mine,
> That were an offering far too small.
> Love so amazing, so divine,
> Demands my soul, my life, my all.

I know a great lady who laughs at life and the time to come. She's a pistol ball. Her mother died at 48, and so at 20 years of age she was left with responsibility for finishing raising a younger brother and caring for a mentally ill father and sister. In mid-life she lost her husband one month and the next month underwent a modified radical mastectomy. Instead of withdrawing from life, within a year she went skiing for the first time in her life to Aspen, Colorado.

She pitched 6 years for her women's softball team and got on stage and clogged with her less than slim body for a community benefit. To a brother-in-law who had to have a piece of his ear cut off to prevent the spread of cancer, she said, "We'll be all right won't we, Royce, as long as we have enough parts left to be cut off?"

She works in the church and sings in the choir, once lead a children's choir, and was treasurer for the building fund for the new social hall. She bought a house adjoining the church property because she was afraid the price might dim the trustees' vision to buy it, and she deeded it to the church. It's in use now by the church.

But until recently she was never asked to say anything about her giving to the church. She was quite reluctant at first, but finally agreed. So for her stewardship witness to the church she said, "My mother died of cancer, but I still had my church. My father was mentally ill for ten years before his death, but all during his illness and after his death, I still had my church. I lost Raymond and buried him from the church, but I still had my church. My children left home for marriage or work and the nest was empty, but guess what! I still had my church. I thank God for my church, and I'm going to support it with all I can now and with some of what I leave after I'm gone." Gratitude!

Quinton Shearouse was a twenty-one year old clean cut crew cut in our Bethesda Church in Effingham County. He drove thirty miles every Sunday to work with our youth group. He had his first job and was tithing, giving forty dollars a week to the church in 1958. At his grandfather's house on Thanksgiving Day he made the mistake of getting on one of these little go-carts to ride it in the yard. It was the first time he'd ever been on one. He got the accelerator confused with the brake and shot out of the yard right in front of a semi on Georgia Highway 17. He was killed instantly—didn't know what hit him.

After the funeral, about a month later, the treasurer of the church told me that Quinton's Daddy, Earl Shearouse, had doubled his pledge and giving to the church. I thought at first when I heard this that his motive must have been a sense of responsibility as a family unit to make up for the loss of that much income to the church. But time showed me otherwise. In the years that followed, whenever any other cause came up, Earl and Lorene, his mother and father, would give and give heavily. They made gifts to Kingdom Builder's Club, Epworth by the Sea, Magnolia Manor, The Methodist Children's Home—you name it.

As I talked to Earl, I discovered that he gave because he enjoyed giving. Now I understand why he doubled his pledge after Quinton's death. In a time of great sorrow, he turned even more to a practice that had never failed to bring him great joy. (II Cor. 8:3, 9:7)

How do we come to be committed people? Gratitude and example!

Now I know you're grateful to me for explaining to you how you happened to wind up with other fine people who are supportive of all Christ's causes. But don't thank me. Thank Peter who said, "For to this you have been called because Christ also suffered for you, leaving you an example that you should follow in his steps."

❖

All Saints Sunday
DID HE SAY A MULTITUDE OF SAINTS?
Matthew 7:13-14, Luke 13:24,29, Revelation 7:9-17

On the First Sunday in November we celebrate All Saints Day that has been going on in the church ever since the 7th Century. Our Roman Catholic forbears had beatified so many saints with special days in those 7 centuries of history that there weren't enough days in the calendar to celebrate the memory of their very special saints. So they compromised by lumping them all together for one grand celebration once a year. But this very problem that they encountered points us to the focus for our thoughts.

We've long had the idea that it was really difficult to become a saint and because it was you'd have very few, certainly not you or me. I guess it's because in one place where Matthew reports his teaching, Jesus focuses on the narrow gate and says, "For the gate is narrow and the road is hard that leads to life, and there are few who find it."

But Luke's memory of that same teaching incident has somebody asking him, "Lord, will only a few be saved?"
And he answers the same way, starting off by saying, "Strive to enter through the narrow door, for many, I tell you, will try to enter and will not be able."

But then down at the end of the story he says, "Then people will come from east and west, from north and south, and will eat in the kingdom of God." Jesus seems to be saying, "Don't limit the vastness of the final number just because it's hard to get in."

So it shouldn't surprise us that John in the Revelation starts his vision of the end of all history with these words, "After this

I looked, and there was a great multitude that no one could count, from every nation, from all tribes and peoples and languages, standing before the throne and before the Lamb, robed in white, with palm branches in their hands."

Did he say a multitude of saints? Yeah! "A great multitude that no one could count." That gives us a chance. We're not just whistling Dixie when we sing, "Lord, I want to be in that number, When the Saints Go Marching In!" It's not the impossible dream when we sing the chorus, "When the Roll is Called Up Yonder, I'll Be There!"

And strangely enough, one of the things that makes it possible is our very memory of these saints that have gone before us. Like Hebrews 12:1 put it, "Since we are surrounded by so great a cloud of witnesses, let us also lay aside every weight and the sin that clings so closely, and let us run with perseverance the race that is set before us."

It would be terrible to have amnesia. The amnesia victim can't remember family name or any of the persons and events that have shaped his or her life and is left with empty, purposeless existence. Somebody said, "If you can't remember any farther back than your own birth, then you are an orphan." So all significant communities recognize the importance of providing collective memory to their offspring.

The Kiawah Indian, Scott Marmaday, tells about how when he was a boy, his father waked him before dawn and took him to the house of an old squaw. He left him there and said, "I'll pick you up tonight."
All day long the old woman told the story of the Kiawah—
How they began near the Yellowstone River,
Why they were such a small tribe,
How they came up out of the river through a hollow log.

How the last one to try to come through the hollow log was a squaw who was pregnant and so she got stuck in the log. So there were no more Kiawah after that. So we're just a small tribe. She explained why they wore the clothes they did. How they survived the terrible winter blizzards. How they were forced out of Kansas onto the Oklahoma Reservation. She sang the songs, she told the stories, and she recited the rituals.

Scott Marmaday said, "I left her house that day a Kiawah." When he graduated from college he got word that the old squaw had died. He took a plane to Bozeman, Montana, rented a car and drove the trail of the Kiawah to her grave. He's a Kiawah.

If you're a Christian today it's because somewhere along the line you've become enrolled in the story. Abraham is your father and Sarah is your mother. Jesus is your brother who died for you. You know about Isaac and Rebecca, Jacob and Rachel and their boys, David and the Psalms the Jews sang. You cry out,

> "If I forget you, O Jerusalem,
> Let my right hand wither!
> Let my tongue cling to the roof of my mouth,
> If I do not remember you."

There are the prophets, the apostles, the Luthers, the Wesleys, the martyrs. There's this "Endless Line of Splendor" in which we find ourselves—the long term Christian community of which we are a part.

But most of us are charged up to get on the course toward the kingdom by the more recent memories of those that have touched our lives in our lifetime and made us what we are. When we come to a Lord's Table most of us become aware of the reality of a doctrine that we say every Sunday in the Apostle's Creed, "the communion of saints." It's not just memory. Just as we believe that when we partake of his body and blood we find the Lord Jesus himself present as host at his table, we also believe that we're not coming up here with just the people in this room.

I remember going back to my hometown, Baxley, to sing at the funeral for their pastor, Raymond Wilder. I looked down at that communion rail before I started to sing and I found myself literally surrounded by a vast throng. I had walked through the church before the funeral. Where the parlor now was I remembered the Primary Class where in a cubbyhole my faith was first awakened by a little older single Sunday School Teacher with an affliction in her voice, deafness in her ears and Jesus in her heart. She had directed me to give away enough frankincense and myrrh in church Christmas pageants to stock the cosmetics counter in an average-sized drug store.

I looked around me in the choir loft and there was not only my mother and father and grandmother, but also Herman the German Iauch, a tenor, who taught me to do tossed salad song leading. We don't go to communion by ourselves. Whom do you meet at this table? Here we meet not just our Lord, but the "Communion of the Saints."

But with all this heritage, what are we called to do? John in the Revelation points out what happened to the martyrs to inspire those living to be faithful. It might be unsaid, but it's implied. "If you're faithful you can join that vast throng about the throne where the Lamb leads them to springs of living water." Sometimes on All Saints Sunday, we start the service with the words of the Hymn; "Come let us join our friends above." Why? Not just for our own sakes. Those who come after us must have some memories. They have to have some more immediate saints with whom to have communion—just like we did.

But even John makes it a little tough for us to imagine ourselves in the role of a saint. As he puts it, (Revelation 7:13-14) "Then one of the elders addressed me, saying, 'Who are these, robed in white, and where have they come from?' I said to him, 'Sir, you are the one that knows.' Then he said to me, 'These are they who have come out of the great ordeal; they have washed their robes and made them white in the blood of the Lamb.'"
That language, "These ... who have come out of the great ordeal"—that's what gives us trouble.

Have you ever listened to a sermon in which the lineup of illustrations were Mother Teresa, Albert Schweitzer, and missionaries who were shot by rebels in the Congo after their supply plane crashed trying to deliver food to starving refugee children? As a young person sitting in church listening to those stories with a few Abraham Lincoln stories thrown in, I just sat there and said to myself, "It's a shame you can't be a Christian in Baxley. Nobody is chasing or imprisoning or killing Christians."

Then under the preaching of Frank Robertson and Tom Whiting at Dooly Camp Meeting, (Dooly by the Wash Hole, not Epworth By the Sea), we closed with "Are Ye Able?" I was a college student leading the song, but I left my song-leading to hit the altar rail and say to God, "I'm Able."
"Are you able to give your life?"
"I'll give my life." And I pictured myself smuggling Bibles through a communist blockade, rescuing a starving child in Africa.

I pictured myself against a gray wall and some soldier saying, "One last chance to deny Christ and live." I confessed my faith, and they said, "Ready, Aim, Fire." The body slumped, the flag was at half-mast, and widows were weeping in the afternoon. Later a monument is built, and people come with their cameras. "Johnny, you stand over there where Hamp gave his life. Let's get your picture."

I was sincere then as I've tried to be these 59 years since then. "I give my life." But nobody warned me that I couldn't write one big check. I've had to write 59 years of little checks: 94 cents, 25 cents, a dollar and ten cents. I've just nibbled away at this giving of life. I hope that's going to be enough.[3]

I can just hope. But do you know what gives me joy on All Saints Day? It's that I know that many of you are joining the company of saints by your life and witness. As you partake of this body and blood, it's no mockery. You're proclaiming the Lord's death until he comes. I've seen so many of my members between a rock and a hard place and I know they're faithful. It's happening now. The Communion of Saints is being enlarged, enhanced, extended and expanded. The Endless Line of Splendor is becoming more endless as we make confession, receive forgiveness and make a commitment to be the people of God in this day.

---

[3] Patterned after one of Fred Craddock's stories on 155 of *Craddock Stories*, but true to my own experience.

Thanksgiving Day/Sunday
A ROCK QUARRY CROSS THANKSGIVING
(Now Thank We All Our God)
Isaiah 51:1-3, Colossians 1:11-20

The mother of two small children ran into another frazzled looking mother at the mall as they both tried to keep up with their children and their packages and she said, "The only thing holding me together is my hair-spray!"

What holds you together? On what do you finally depend to give some structure and meaning to your life when everything else seems to be falling apart around you? Cultural Historian Ray Browne said, "We have always had two or three Rocks of Gibraltar we could count on: the church, the bank, and the law. We can't count on any of these now. No wonder we are frustrated and awfully gloomy." Like every prophetic statement this seems to be a little overdrawn, but can we deny that the church has priests who molest children while demanding stringent sexual standards of others, preachers who abscond with the hard-earned contributions of the faithful, and pastors who exploit the counselor-client relation? Can we deny that some banks bilk the customer and go bankrupt, but still count on that same misused public to bail them out? Can we deny that the law is sometimes used to put down the poor and protect the powerful who seem to be able to operate above or outside the law?

So with the demise of all these, what keeps you going? What holds you together? If you are able to withstand the onslaught of all these forces that would pull us apart, you're a survivor! How are you doing it?

There were some awfully discouraged people once. They were not unemployed, or underemployed. If anything, they were over-employed because their homes and cities had been destroyed and they had been carried off into slavery. But they were survivors. They became the famous "remnant" that came back to rebuild Jerusalem and the temple and their life together as a worshipping people. Isaiah has God saying to them, "Listen to me, you that pursue righteousness, you that seek the Lord. Look to the rock from which you were hewn, and to the quarry from which you were dug. Look to Abraham your father and to Sarah who bore you; for he was but one when I called him, but I blessed and made him many."

This is the first clue to what holds you together—"Look to the rock from which you were hewn." Look to Abraham and Sarah. Look back to your roots. Look back to the overarching purpose of your life. What did God say to Abraham when God called him? "I will bless you, and make your name great, so that you will be a blessing... And in you all the families of the earth shall be blessed." You people are not really here for yourselves and what you can get for yourselves. So you have some tough times for yourselves? Remember the overarching purpose of your lives as the people of God, and it'll bring you through. "And joy and gladness will be found in you, thanksgiving and the voice of song."(Genesis 12:3ff.)

This is really the rock from which you were hewn—to be here for others. That old Gospel song from the Broadman Hymnal that went "Make me a blessing... out of my life may Jesus shine!" That's it! That's what keeps people going. How did Mother Teresa, that woman in her eighties, keep the energy and endurance to keep going for God and become the best-known woman in the whole world? Could it have been her motto? You know what it was? "Let the Jesus in me serve the Jesus in you."

A lot of our Methodist Churches are building Habitat for Humanity houses now. What keeps something like Habitat for Humanity going—non-profit, labor intensive, for those who participate? Will Willimon who is now a Bishop was Dean of the Chapel at Duke University and was visiting with a Duke student that had spent a semester in Americus, Georgia building homes with and for the poor. He said, "What was your time there like?"

She said, "Americus is really small. There's nothing to do there at night except to go to a Gospel Sing at some little church. The college students who are there with Habitat do a lot of sitting on the porch in the evenings. We just have a beer and sit and talk."

Will said, "Millard Fuller doesn't mind if you have a beer?" She said, "Well, I guess he sort of looks the other way, but you can't sleep with each other!"

Will teased her a little. He said, "Really? Is that because Millard is a Baptist instead of a Methodist? Doesn't he want people to have a good time?"

She said, "No, I don't think so. Millard says that there are just too many poor people without adequate housing for us to be wasting time." It's the overarching purpose when we look to the rock from which we were hewn. "By you shall all the families of the earth bless themselves!"

But Isaiah gives another clue as to what holds us together. He has God saying, "look to the quarry from which you were dug." I think that this is more than Jewish poetic parallelism:

"Look to the rock from which you were hewn
And to the quarry from which you were dug."

This is different from two parallel phrases that mean exactly the same thing. For me, the rock and the quarry are a little different. The rock is that family of which we are a part and its overarching purpose; but the quarry speaks of the hard knocks and the crushing blows through which the family has gone. This is the crucible that formed our character to bring us to be the people we are now. These are the mistakes we made, the sins we committed for which we received forgiveness, the tough things we went through that made us what we are as survivors.

I remember one Thanksgiving sermon at Wesley Monumental, I told about how I was raised in Baxley, Georgia with a mentally ill father and a mother who died after a double mastectomy when I was just sixteen. I told how I sold papers at the hotels at six o'clock in the mornings from the time I was ten years old to help make ends meet. But the ends would keep growing farther apart. When I finished that little recital, Cecil Abarr, the head of the Branigar Corporation, came up to me afterward and said, "Hamp, you want to have a contest on telling "poor" stories? I can match you story for story." And the truth is that nearly all of us remember the quarry from which we were dug.

About this quarry—at the time we're going through it with the pounding, and the crushing, and the hewing, and the shaping, it doesn't make any sense to us. It's only with perspective that we come to see it. That's why God says, "Look to the quarry from which you were dug." When you do that, as strange as it seems, you might be able to come to "thanksgiving and the voice of song." Go back over your life. Can you remember the quarry from which you were dug?

In LAKE WOEBEGON DAYS by Garrison Keillor, the last paragraph says: "Some luck lies in not getting what you thought you wanted, but getting what you have, which, once you have it, you may be smart enough to see, is what you would have wanted had you known." Many of us have been held together because we looked to the rock from which we were hewn and the quarry from which we were dug. But we haven't yet pointed to the most powerful force for holding anyone together.

At the heart of his Colossian hymn to Christ the King, Paul says, "He himself is before all things and in him all things hold together." He's the glue that keeps the universe coherent, so that things don't fall apart. An effective government, then as now, maintains a working social order, protects people from external threats, keeps the economy functioning and makes the trains and planes run on time. In short, good government holds everything together. And if Jesus is truly our ruler and holds first place in our hearts, he holds us together.

That "first place" business is the key. Paul says, he's "the first-born from the dead, so that he might come to have first place in everything." Now, we do a lot of talking about first place in our culture. Several years ago when I was District Superintendent of the Savannah District, I was out at Wilmington Island United Methodist Church on a Communion Sunday morning. I was just dropping in unannounced to see how things were going in that congregation and to hear their preacher. I got a bonus. It was during the time that Herschel Walker was doing his heroics at the University of Georgia and the Bulldogs had been declared national champions. During the children's sermon, the pastor, Jim Jensen, threw open his black robe to reveal underneath a Red and Black T-shirt with the caption emblazoned—"WE'RE NUMBER 1!" It may be a harmless exercise in adolescent exuberance on the football field, but who is really #1?

The answer to that question gives us perspective on who we are and where we are. When the word came down that the Corps of Engineers might lay off vast numbers or even close the Savannah office, one who was threatened was heard to say, "I don't know who I am or where I am." It's understandable. We often get our meaning in life from our job and how we rank in our job—whether that income enables us to move up in our circles and buy a new home in the right part of town and be somebody, moving up toward #1.

But the reason people like this are not totally destroyed, and the reason they hold together is because they know the one who has come to have first place in everything, "and in him all things hold together." Because they have looked to the rock from which they were hewn, they know that ultimately they've been blessed and put here to be a blessing to others, and they know that God is not going to go back on that promise. For as Paul puts it, you're "made strong with all the strength that comes from his glorious power," and you're "prepared to endure everything with patience, while joyfully giving thanks to the Father, who has enabled you to share in the inheritance of the saints in the light."

It helps us to remember who we are and where we are—that we're not those who have to get meaning by winning out over others economically or any other way. How did He get to be # 1? Was it by battering brutally through the line? Did he overpower his opponents with crushing force? Paul just says, "through Him God was pleased to reconcile to himself all things, whether on earth or in heaven, by making peace through the blood of his cross." He's #1 in vulnerable, dying love for others so that in Him all things might hold together. The armies of this eternal king are all foot soldiers with bleeding feet who carry not a sword, but a cross.

Garrison Keillor who reminisces about his rural growing up days in Minnesota told once about a memorable Thanksgiving dinner. He said it was ruined because his Aunt Zelda had been nibbling too much during the preparations for the feast, and when they got to the table, before they even had the blessing, she became ill and delayed their beginning.

Then after they'd cleaned up as best they could, they made the mistake of calling on Uncle Gunder for the blessing. Oblivious to how ravenous everybody was he launched into his typical thanksgiving to God for all their forebears whose names he called like in one of the genealogies in the Bible—on through every current family and kissing cousin there around the table. He concluded with a long treatise on our gratitude to God for his salvation of all of us by the death of his Son, making peace through the blood of his cross.

When he reached this point, he just broke into tears of joy. Garrison's final comment on this went something like this: "Now, all of us knew all that—that Jesus had died for us and that God was using him to bring us all together and to reconcile us to each other and to himself by the blood of his cross. But the difference was, I guess, that Uncle Gunder just never had gotten over it."

As you celebrate Thanksgiving, will you look to the rock from which you were hewn and to the quarry from which you were dug? Will you let him "have first place in everything?" Will you let the one in whom all things hold together hold you together, too? Will you give thanks for rock, quarry and cross? Or have you gotten over all that?

Rest now in the name of God, the creator, who "has rescued us from the power of darkness and transferred us into the kingdom of his beloved Son, in whom we have redemption, the forgiveness of sins."

First Sunday in Advent
ABOUT WHERE GOD IS THIS SEASON
Matthew 2:13-18, Romans 13:11-14

"Besides this, you know what time it is; how it is now the moment for you to wake from sleep. For salvation is nearer to us now than when we became believers. The night is far gone; the day is near. Let us then lay aside the works of darkness and put on the armor of light. Let us live honorably as in the day, not in reveling and drunkenness, not in debauchery and licentiousness, not in quarreling and jealousy.

Instead, put on the Lord Jesus Christ, and make no provision for the flesh, to gratify its desires."

How many sermons do you think are going to be preached on this passage of Scripture from Matthew about the Slaughter of the Innocents this Christmas? A dozen, a thousand, tens of thousands? Or do you guess that you're probably the only people that are going to be afflicted with such a choice for an Advent/Christmas message. Poor us! This intrudes into the comfort and joy of the Christmas season in disturbing fashion, as a quick rereading of Matthew 2:13-18 will demonstrate. Why this is a time for sentimentality over shepherds, or recitals about "the romance of the manger," or starry-eyed stanzas about the star in the East. Baldly stated, this story confronts us with an appalling fact—the price of the birth of the babe in Bethlehem was the slaughter of hundreds of other babies in Bethlehem and elsewhere. For every shepherd who was thrilled by an angel song, a hundred mothers wept bitter tears.

When our son Wade sang in the Emory Glee Club, on the first Friday night in Advent they always put on the Festival of Nine Lessons and Carols. After the reading of each lesson, whoever was reading would say, "Thanks be to God." The eighth lesson was read by Dean Judson Ward. He read the passage about how Herod in a furious rage sent and killed all the male children who were two years old and under. Right after he finished that passage, he said, "Thanks be to God."

After the service, somebody pointed out to me the incongruity of what he had done. You can't say, "Thanks be to God" right after you talk about how a madman has killed a bunch of innocent babies. At the time I explained it by saying, "Well it was just the rote response. He wasn't thanking God that children were killed... but just 'Thanks be to God' that we can read and hear his Word." It was only the ritual response at the closing of the reading of a passage of Scripture. But you know the more I have thought about that passage and the response, "Thanks be to God," the more I realize how appropriate it is to say it... especially to us in Advent 2012.

For the whole story says that God chooses to send his son and his love even into a world where people go mad with paranoia—unreasoning fear and hatred—and cause innocent children to die. You remember how in 1978, 913 followers of Jim Jones and the Peoples Temple committed a mass suicide in northern Guyana at a site called, Jonestown? It was in the beginning of Advent, near Christmas that they followed their leader to drink the Koolaid laced with cyanide. One of the rescue workers at the scene of the carnage said, "Picking up the bodies of the children was what got to me the most."

Oh we don't thank God that children died or that Jim Jones and his kind perished in their madness. But we thank God that not even the madness and meanness of Herod could shut him out. We thank God that not even the madness of the sectarian violence in Iraq and Afghanistan that kills innocent families can shut him out. When our own boys and girls are shipped back in body bags... when the genocide in Darfur is sponsored by their own Sudanese government... none of these can shut God and his love out.

"Thanks be to God" for a faith that knows God sends his son to be with us in the midst of the madness of our time.

We couldn't stand it otherwise. We couldn't take "The Slaughter of the Innocents" if we didn't know about another slaughter. I guess that's why the church always celebrates the Lord's Supper on the first Sunday in Advent. It would be quite intolerable, both to the imagination and to the Christian conscience, were it not for another thing that enables us to read the Slaughter of the Innocents and still worship the God whose birth in human life is celebrated by that gruesome spectacle. This is the fact that the baby whose birth occasioned the slaughter of the other babies received exactly the same kind of treatment himself. In his case it was postponed. For, not many years later and not very far away, there was another gruesome spectacle: the Slaughter of the Innocent, the Innocent One whose only crime was that he loved too much. We can stand the Slaughter of the Innocents only because the God who permitted it did not exempt himself from the same kind of treatment. He exacts of us nothing to which he is not also willing to submit himself.

This is what makes the Christmas story—the Slaughter of the Innocents included—such a radical challenge to conventional faith in 2012. It doesn't promise that God will exempt us from the ugly realities of existence. It only promises us—and the promise is everything—that he'll meet those realities with us, sharing the awful burdens that humanity in a fallen world must shoulder. If this weren't so we'd have a God who didn't care, who could turn his back on his children in distress; and on such a God we would feel justified in turning our backs. But since he does care and, therefore, shares with us all that life inflicts on us, whether good or bad, we know that nothing of our pain and sorrow can be alien to him. We also know that his involvement in our pain and sorrow transforms them so that rather than being threats to the reality of his love, they become vehicles through which his love is expressed as healing power.

So where is God in this season? Could he have been in the Macon City Council meeting where they passed an ordinance to outlaw panhandlers and beggars on the streets, and a courageous pastor spoke up to say, "It's tempting to legislate them out of town, but that would be a grave mistake. The church should stand on the side of those who have the least in our society." That pastor's church along with our help was "putting its money where his mouth was," Macon Outreach at Mulberry with its soup kitchen feeds about 150 of our poorest citizens every day.

Oh we're sympathetic with business people who think trade will be driven away. And any of us who've ever dealt with the bolder ones among the poor know that SOME FEW of them are professional con artists preying on our sympathy. But could it be that in the midst of all our spending on ourselves and our affluent loved ones, we don't want to be reminded by these "not so pure" representatives that there is still a world of hunger out there? That might be uncomfortable. It's almost as bad as Paul trying to spoil the season by saying, "Put on the Lord Jesus Christ, and make no provision for the flesh, to gratify its desires."

Some time ago, Bono, lead singer for the popular group, U2, spoke to a Prayer Breakfast in Washington. This is what he said: "God is in the slums, in the cardboard boxes where the poor play house. God is in the silence of a mother who has infected her child with a virus that will end both their lives. God is in the cries heard under the rubble of war. God is in the debris of wasted opportunity and lives. And God is with us, if we are with them."

A reporter observed a food distribution at a mission. Here's his account of the event: The line was long but moving briskly and in that line at the very end stood a young girl about twelve years of age. She waited patiently as those at the front of that long line received a little rice, some canned goods or a little fruit. Slowly but surely she was getting closer to the front of that line—closer to the food. From time to time she would glance across the street. She didn't notice the growing concern on the faces of those distributing the food. The food was running out. Their anxiety began to show but she didn't notice. Her attention seemed always to focus on three figures under the trees across the street.

At long last she stepped forward to get her food but the only thing left was one lonely banana. The workers were almost ashamed to tell her that was all that was left. She didn't seem to mind. In fact she seemed genuinely happy to get that solitary banana. Quietly she took the precious gift and ran across the street where three small children waited—perhaps her sisters and a brother. Very deliberately she peeled the banana and very carefully divided the banana into three equal parts, placing the precious food in the eager hands of those three younger ones. "One for you, one for you, one for you." She then sat down and licked the inside of that banana peel.

The reporter said, "When I saw her lick the inside of that banana peel, I swear I saw the face of God."

In the story of the Slaughter of the Innocents, Matthew tells us, "Rachel, weeping for her children... refused to be consoled." But to us, weeping for our children and for our sin-sick world, the word of consolation has come, and the circumstance of Jesus' death becomes the means by which we bear the circumstance of Jesus' birth. Think on these things as we begin the journey to Bethlehem.

❖

Christmas Eve/Day
LOOKING FOR SIGNS IN THE WRONG PLACES
Luke 2:1-20, Text-2:12
"And this shall be a sign unto you; ye shall find the babe wrapped in swaddling clothes, lying in a manger."

Are you struck by the fact that this so-called sign is astonishingly unpretentious? You'd think the sign would be the appearance of the angel/messenger himself/herself. You'd think at the least the real sign that God had come to earth was the multitude of the heavenly hosts praising God and singing, "Glory to God in the highest!"

But the sign is not an angel. The sign is not even a song. The sign is not a noise of any kind. "How silently, how silently, the wondrous gift is given." The noisiest part of it might have been the whimper of a baby's cry, for it was on a "Silent night, Holy night" that he was born. It seems so remarkable to me that when God comes to speak God's word to us, that Word becomes a child. A child announced by singing, not by thunder. A child born by lamplight in silent night, rather than a Word that shakes the mountains, pouring rivers of unstoppable fire down every side. The Word comes not with violence but in the vulnerability of a little child, a mewling, gurgling, diapered, dimpled baby. This was the sign! What a surprise!

But humankind has always had trouble seeing the real signs. You remember in Genesis (28:16) how Jacob had cheated his brother Esau out of his birthright and was running from him to save his life. He wearily lies down to rest and can find nothing but a stone to put under his head. He dreams of a ladder set up on the earth with the top of it reaching to heaven. (Remember, "We are Climbing Jacob's ladder.") And God speaks to him in this dream and says, "All the families of the earth shall be blessed in you and your offspring." He woke from his sleep, and what would we have said? We would have thought, "No wonder I had nightmares--anybody that tries to use a rock for a pillow must have rocks in his head. Sure! God's gonna make something out of me! Uh huh. Why it's only a matter of time until Esau catches up to me and it will be 'Goodbye, brother!' I just must be scared out of my wits."

But that isn't what Jacob said. With all his faults, the God-sensitive Jacob was somehow able to read the signs. When he woke from sleep he said, (28:16) "Surely the Lord is in this place and I did not know it." And he was afraid then sure enough and said, (17) "How awesome is this place!" (I guess this is where our young people get their saying which they utter about every other sentence these days, "It was awesome!") Jacob said, "How awesome is this place! This is none other than the house of God and this is the gate of heaven!"

On several occasions in the scripture the Pharisees and Sadducees came to Jesus and asked him for a sign from heaven to indicate his authority. He told them, Mt. 16:2-3, "When it is evening, you say it will be fair weather, for the sky is red. and threatening." (Where did you think we got that saying, 'Red sky at night, sailors delight. Red sky in the morning, sailors take warning?') Jesus said, "You know how to interpret the appearance of the sky, but you cannot interpret the signs of the times." He went on to say that it's' an evil and adulterous generation that asks for a sign beyond those signs that have already been given to it... if we would only look and listen.

Do you remember the encounter between Mary, who was pregnant with Jesus, and her cousin Elizabeth, who was pregnant with John the Baptist? Most women six or seven months pregnant who felt a child kick in her womb when her pregnant cousin came in the door would have said, "Mary, I must be carrying some kind of precocious child here." Few would have thought to say like Elizabeth, Luke 2:42-44, "Blessed are you among women, and blessed is the fruit of your womb. And why has this happened to me that the mother of my Lord comes to me? For as soon as I heard the sound of your greeting, the child in my womb leaped for joy." The scripture explains it by saying, vs. 40, "Elizabeth was filled with the Holy Spirit." You see, we rarely see the signs on our own. We keep looking for signs in the wrong places.

We have a hard enough time spotting greatness in people, much less seeing God hidden in the ordinary. A professor at Princeton University was walking by a local inn in Princeton and a woman saw him and mistook him for a bellboy. She summoned him to carry her luggage into the inn. He turned immediately, followed her instructions, and received a small tip for his services, and he pocketed it. Then Albert Einstein made his way on to his office to probe and ponder the secrets of the universe. The most celebrated intellect of our time, serving. Sometimes it's hard to see the signs.

In a little country store in Hodginville, Kentucky in the winter of 1809, a farmer said to the proprietor who was trying to stay warm around a pot-bellied stove, "Ezra, is there anythin' goin' on around here? What's happening?"

Ezra said, "Nothin' atall, nothin' atall. Ceptin' for a baby boy born down to Tom Lincoln's last night. You know his momma, Tom's wife, that Nancy Hanks woman, you know she's an illegitimate herself. I'd say that baby ain't got much of a chance in this world… cain't amount to much. What do ya' think?" It's hard to see the signs. It would be a lot easier if we were as fortunate as the shepherds and had an angel to tell us where to look.

I can hear two male schoolteachers talking in the teacher's lounge on their coffee break in Milwaukee, Wisconsin in 1921. One says, "Did you hear what that crazy Golda[4] did? She's

---

[4] Golda Meir who became the first female Prime Minister of Israel.

thrown it all away. She was one of our best teachers here at the
high school, and some people say she might have even made
principal if she had stayed. Pretty good for a little Ruskie Jew
immigrant, if you ask me. But I knew her wild ideas would
finally destroy her. She's going to immigrate to Palestine. She's
caught up in that crazy Zionist movement. Now she'll never
amount to anything." Don't you know the Meirs are just
broken-hearted? But that's what happens when women get so
uppity and won't stay in their place." Oh for an angel to help
us see the signs!

Have you guessed by now that I'm going to try to sneak up
on you in your thought and suggest that maybe we're missing
seeing Jesus alive and at work in our time? Gregory McGill,
one of our Methodist pastors out in Texas, collects Last Supper
scenes and four of them grace his parsonage. He says: When
my daughter was two years old, she learned that the central
figure in the picture is Jesus. She was unable to pronounce his
name correctly, and would say "Geezuh." She got me to
playing a little game with her. She'd have me pick her up and
take her to one of the scenes. She'd then point to the central
figure and say, "Geezuh." Then she'd say, "Find more
Geezuh." Then I'd have to carry her to see another picture of
the Last Supper where the process would repeat itself. Greg
says, "My daughter's phrase, 'find more Geezuh' is what being
Christian is all about." As we progress in discipleship, we
should all have the desire to "find more Jesus."

In medieval times there was a charming legend that said that
on Christmas Eve the Christ Child wandered throughout the
world, looking for places where he would be welcomed. Those
who loved him, hoping that he might find their homes, placed
lighted candles in the window to invite him in.

No one, of course, knew for sure in what guise the Christ
Child might appear. Perhaps he would come dressed in the

rags of a beggar, or he might come as a poor and lonely child. He might also appear incognito in the form of the disabled, the halt and the blind, who were put out to roam the streets in medieval cities. I guess that's why we do it now. We're just following the historical pattern.

So it became customary for devout Christians to welcome into their homes all who knocked at their doors on Christmas Eve. To turn any away may have meant the rejection of the Christ Child, who had come in an unfamiliar garb. During the Advent Season we remember that the Christ Child is wandering along our streets, looking for homes where he will be given warmth and shelter. The Candles in the windows of our homes, the lighting of the Advent Wreath, candles in our church windows, in our offering for the poor and homeless, and the lighting of all our candles following communion that we often do symbolizes to all of our community that Christ is our guest. Here is a warm and welcoming place where there is room for him.

That should be sign enough to set our souls on fire for God... to call us all to our knees in adoration and repentance at some communion altar on Christmas Eve or at our place of Worship on Christmas Sunday.

FAVORITE STORIES FROM ALL MY BOOKS

Bishop C. W. Hancock, whom we know as "Handy" said, "When I was the pastor at Mulberry Street Church, Macon, Mrs. Orville Park was a member of the church. She was a most interesting person. At the time she was in her late nineties. Yet, she was very mentally alert. When I visited her in her home on Orange Street, I found that she was most conversant about current events. She listened to the news. She read the newspaper regularly. She kept up with everything.

Mrs. Park was in and out of the hospital. On a visit to see her during one of those times, she remarked to me: 'Brother Hancock, I do hope that I do not die in one of these hospital gowns.'

I asked her why she had that thought. Her reply was, 'I'd hate to spend eternity backing around in heaven.' Great sense of humor for a woman nearing 100 years of age."[5]

When Johnny Deas was pastor of the Leary Circuit, he reported having to drive back to the parsonage at Leary from the Church at Damascus. He said, "I noticed as I left Damascus that the gas gauge showed empty. As I drove toward home, I remembered that the speedometer and the odometer were both broken on that old car. When I got back to the parsonage, I thought about that situation.

Before I left Damascus, where no gas stations were open, the gas gauge told me that I couldn't go anywhere. As I was traveling, the speedometer told me that I wasn't going anywhere. When I arrived at the parsonage, the odometer told

---

[5] From *Little Stories/Big Ideas, p.5*

me that I hadn't been anywhere. But the greater reality was that I was at home."[6]

When my friend, Bill Dupree, was pastor of the Winona Park Methodist Church in Waycross, there was a faithful couple, Hugh and Roselyn Farrior, in the church. They had four young boys. Roselyn's first husband was killed in an automobile accident, leaving her with two boys. Hugh's first wife had died, leaving him with one son. They met, married, and God blessed their home with a fourth son. She told Bill how she was dating another man before she met Hugh. Frequently she told her two small boys, who wanted a daddy so badly, to pray and God would send them the daddy they needed. She was feeling them out one day and asked them how they'd like to have the man she was dating as their daddy.

Oldest one said, "Let's wait and see who Jesus sends." Needless to say, she didn't marry him. She waited and married Hugh.

I remember George Wright, our former Conference Lay Leader from Tifton, telling about the guy who went into a crossroads country store and found a woebegone storeowner hanging over the counter looking like he'd just lost his last friend. Behind him there was just shelf after shelf full of Morton's Salt. That's all he had on his shelves. The stranger said, "Friend, you must sell a lot of Morton's salt."

He said, "No, I don't sell much Morton's salt. But that fellow that sold me—he sells a lot of Morton's salt!"[7]

The old Preacher-Philosopher Charlie Ledbetter, of our Conference, fought catarrh when he spoke. When Guy Hutcherson introduced him to me, while I was a student at

---

[6] From *Little Stories/Big Ideas, p.8*
[7] From *Little Stories/Big Ideas, p.16*

Candler, the first thing he said to me was, "Son, harumph! harumph! Can you say 'Bob,' without putting your lips together?"

I tried mightily, but I couldn't and said, "No, Brother Ledbetter."

He solemnly put his forefinger between his lips and said, "Bob!"

It was from Brother Charlie that I first learned about the law of the necessary minimum that we apply in much of our lives. Somebody asked Brother Ledbetter, when he was serving at Rhine, Georgia, why he hadn't married again after his wife died. He said, "Next woman I marry will have to be as rich as Mrs. Rockefeller, as pious as Susannah Wesley and as pretty as Mae West."

But most men are content with less. Does she love me? Can she cook and run a family? And, these days, "Can she earn half or more of the living?" Can she keep her mouth shut long enough for me to tell her all of my problems? Then I'll marry her! I know enough. This is the law of the necessary minimum.

I don't want to be flippant about a serious subject, but what about the things that happen that make no sense—the tragic things in life? Why is there calamity, why insanity, why cancer, why polio, why birth defects, why tsunamis? I don't know. I only know the character of our great God can be utterly trusted. God is love and cannot be false to God's nature, and I count on that. This is the necessary minimum for living. The secret things belong unto the Lord our God, but the things which are revealed belong unto us and to our children forever. Is that enough? Is that enough for you? I hope so.[8]

I ran into The Reverend T. O. Lambert at Conference one year. At that time he was over eighty and working as a

---

[8] From *Little Stories/Big Ideas, p.21*

Retired Associate Pastor at St Luke in Columbus. I said, "How are you doing, Brother Lambert?"

He said, "My voice hasn't cracked, and it doesn't quaver. My memory hasn't failed and my steps don't totter. I haven't lost my interest in people, and I haven't lost my faith in God."[9]

Joe Cresson, a columnist for: the Louisville Courier-Journal, tells a story about a man in eastern Kentucky, who went to the doctor. As he sat in the doctor's office, he said, he studied the face of a man across the room. "The more I looked at him," he said, "the more I knowed I knowed him. An', what's more, I could tell by the way he was a-starin' at me, he knowed that he knowed me. Well, we set there a-lookin' at each other, knowin' we knowed one another, and finally I decided I was gonna' get up and go over and make sure I knowed him. An' about that time he decided to get up and come over to make sure he knowed me. So we come to the center of the room to make sure we knowed one another, an', you know what? 'Twarn't neither of us!"[10]

Since we finished the book with Advent and Christmas Messages, let's end with a favorite Christmas Story.

When the people on my street put up their outdoor Christmas decorations, it made me think of this family that had the custom of putting large plywood letters bordered with Christmas lights on their roof each year. The letters spelled "NOEL." It was an unusual piece of decoration. One year the father was a little slow in getting the letters up on the roof. Finally, late one Saturday afternoon in mid-December, he got the project under way. The letters were large and hard to handle. It was a very windy afternoon, and he was heard to mutter some rather "unchristmasy" comments under his breath as he struggled with the large plywood letters. When

---

[9] From *Little Stories/Big Ideas, p. 35*
[10] From *Little Stories/Big Ideas, p.75*

at last he finished he climbed down the ladder triumphantly, instructing the children to plug in the lights. When the lights came on and blazed against the dark sky, everybody rolled in laughter. He had put the letters backwards. Instead of "NOEL" he had spelled "LEON."

I never did learn what the errant father said or did about the situation, but I think I might have left the letters just as they were. Very few people know what "NOEL" means, though we sing it each year, but everybody knows somebody named "LEON." If Leon came by and saw his name in lights on a house, I am sure he would be touched. You see the deepest meaning of Christmas is captured in this merry mystery when it's suddenly revealed that God is interested in people like Leon. I'm sure that this was a part of Paul's sense of what was happening when Jesus came. Doesn't he say, "now revealed… so that all nations might believe and obey him?"[11]

---

[11] From *A Christmas Cornucopia, p.51*